A BEER
IN THE LOIRE

A BEER
IN THE LOIRE

Tommy Barnes

MUSWELL
PRESS

First published by Muswell Press in 2018

Typeset by M Rules
Copyright © Tommy Barnes 2018

Tommy Barnes asserts the moral right
to be identified as the author of this work.

Printed and bound by CPI Group (UK) Ltd, Croydon CR0 4YY.

ISBN: 9781999613563

Muswell Press
London
N6 5HQ
www.muswell-press.co.uk

For George and Ellen Barnes

BEER NO. 1:
Mud-Coloured IPA

RECIPE	MISTAKES
6 kg Maris Otter malt	Lack of clearing agent (Irish moss)
500 g German pilsner malt	Failure to take a gravity reading post-boil
40 g Nugget hops at start of boil	Fermentation at wrong temperature for the yeast
20 g Citra hops after 75 minutes	Failure to rack beer before bottling
20 g Citra hops after 85 minutes	Getting distracted by dogs eating each other's vomit
20 g Citra hops post-boil for 10 minutes	Brewing in nothing but Y-fronts

B urt leered at me – squat, beer-bellied, surly, defiant, a cigar butt protruding from the corner of his chubby, English-hating face. He had stolen my wallet, but I had cut him off in the front garden before he could escape and I was currently working out how hard I should hit him with a spade. There'll be apologists out there saying

'Violence doesn't solve anything' and 'You shouldn't take the law into your own hands' and 'He's only a nine-week-old puppy – don't hit him with a spade,' but you weren't there, guys. You were not there. This was the culmination of a week of psychological warfare and, up until now, Burt had been winning comfortably, thanks to a couple of sensational coups: two days before, he had chewed open my cigar box and hidden the cigars around the garden and today he'd stolen my wallet from my back pocket while I was bending over to get him some food. He was a raving sociopath.

Rose, my girlfriend, called me from the upstairs landing. 'Tommy, I think you should come and see this.'

'Hold on, I'm going to hit Burt with a spade,' I said.

'He's a nine-week-old puppy.'

'People said that about Hitler.'

'Nobody said that about Hitler. Leave him alone and come and see this.'

'OK. Fine. I'm going to throw him as high as I can into a tree.'

'Don't throw him into a tree. Come and see this.'

I hissed at Burt, who eyeballed me with contempt and continued chewing his cigar butt. I could still feel his eyes on the back of my head as I walked through the front door to see Damien, our French neighbour, prowling the walls of the living room with a spectacular electric drill in his hands. Before I could question him, Rose called again from upstairs: 'Hurry up and look at this.'

It's probably a land prawn, I thought. That's what Rose called the large, crustacean-like centipedes that turned up on the walls every now and then. She hadn't quite come to terms with French countryside insects yet, but when I

2

arrived on the landing there was no land prawn. Instead, she was standing by the window looking into the Richelieu Forest opposite our house.

'I tell you what, Rose, I'm going to have that little shit deported.'

'You can't deport Burt. He's actually French, unlike you.'

'Wrong. He's half Australian sheepdog. I'm going to get him sent back to the colonies. He's driving me mad. Shit. I think I'm having a breakdown. The walls feel like they are shaking. Oh no, Rose. I can hear a buzzing. I'm having a stroke. This is Burt's fault.'

'You're not having a stroke. The walls are shaking because Damien's drilling a hole in our wall.'

'He's doing what?'

'He said you'd agreed to it last night when they came round for dinner.'

I thought back to the previous night, sitting by the fire, drinking a bottle of Cognac with Damien and Celia, our French neighbours. It was the first time we'd met them, having only bought our new house a couple of weeks previously. Damien, mid-twenties, tall and thin, a hand-rolled cigarette hanging out of his mouth and tightly curled black hair sprouting haphazardly from his head, was staring at the fireplace while I poured him another half a pint of Cognac.

'You see, the problem is your fire doesn't get enough oxygen,' he said. Damien spoke French slowly and deliberately for our benefit. 'If I drill a hole here, then your fire would work better.' His finger circled clumsily before he saw through his double vision and settled on a spot on the wall next to the fireplace. I agreed instantly.

'One must teach the walls who's boss.' I nodded to myself

3

sagely as I guzzled my fifth brandy and dropped in and out of consciousness.

'*D'accord*, Tommy. I will come round on Monday and drill it,' said Damien.

'Brilliant! Drilling holes. That's living.'

And that's how we left it. I didn't actually think he would do it. I always promise to do things when I am drunk but I don't actually do them. It must be a French thing.

'Hold on, Rose. But if Damien is down there drilling a giant hole in the living-room wall, then . . . then aren't we going to have a giant hole in the living-room wall?'

Before she could answer, I charged back downstairs. Damien was packing his drill back into the case. There was a hole fifteen centimetres in diameter in the wall next to our fireplace. I sat down. From the sofa I could now see our garden. Burt ran past the hole chewing my bank card.

'It's OK, I did it for free because we are neighbours,' Damien said as he strolled out of the front door, adding, 'maybe get a grille to stop the mice.'

'Right. Good idea. Thanks, Damien,' I said.

Rose sat down beside me. Together we stared into the hole.

'That's just what we need. It's winter, we can't afford to heat the house and now we have a giant hole in the wall. Why did you call me, anyway?' I said.

Rose handed me a pregnancy test. I was puzzled for a moment until I zeroed in on a distinct blue line two thirds of the way up.

'Oh God, no. Oh no. A baby? But we can't afford a baby. Send it back!' I said.

'Aren't you happy?'

I was happy, of course I was happy, but we'd only been

4

trying for a few weeks. I'd expected, perfectly reasonably, that if my sperm were as *laissez-faire* as the rest of me, it would take at least a year before they ran out of excuses for doing any work and got round to making babies, and by then we would have figured out how to make a living, and by then perhaps we'd have lost Burt to a tragic steamrolling accident.

I shut my eyes and inhaled slowly, trying to stay calm. Instead, the image of a wood-panelled digital alarm clock appeared on the back of my eyelids. It was the old 1980s alarm clock from my nan's flat in Bethnal Green. However, it wasn't telling the time any more. It was counting down. The numbers were counting down so fast that they were a blur. I used to love that alarm clock as a child. Now it had become a harbinger of some terrifying unknown.

'Yes, no, I am really happy. We're going to have a baby! Oh, dear God. But we haven't got any money, Rose. We bought a house that was twice our budget, I still can't find anyone to publish my novel and our redundancy money has all but run out.'

'Don't worry, Tommy. You'll get a publisher one day. And anyway, once you get your brewery off the ground we'll be all right.'

'The brewery? Oh yes, the *brewery*. No, you're quite right. Just got to get that off the ground and we'll be OK. We're having a baby!' we held each other for a few moments. I shut my eyes and the wood-panelled clock sprung up again. 'Right. I suppose I'd better pop out and brew some beer.'

My plan to make a new life in France was multifaceted, you see. Only a fool would leave a perfectly good office job in London and move to rural France, basing their entire financial future on writing a bestselling debut comedy/crime novel. No, I had a second prong to my idiot fork.

5

I would also start a brewery. In one of the finest wine-producing areas in France. Indeed, in an area in which, as far as I could see, the locals had absolutely no particular interest in drinking beer. Not only this, but somewhere in my meticulous planning I had overlooked the tiny detail that in order to make beer you *actually needed to know how to brew beer.*

Leaving Rose bemused in the living room, a determined wind blowing through the hole in the wall, I walked into the front garden and stared accusingly at the house, cursing my surprisingly effective testicles. Then I went round to the back barn, hauled open the giant old wooden doors and circled my beer-brewing machine. I hadn't told Rose I didn't know how to brew beer. As far as she knew, I'd been in the barn these past few days conducting research and testing, not slumped next to a large metal cylinder with my head in my hands.

The cylinder was called the GrainFather. I had bought it from the internet on the advice of my friend Chris, who knows about making beer. He told me to buy it because, having come to know me over a number of years, he was fully aware that I was a moron in a variety of different and ever more surprising ways, and therefore I would only be able to operate the most user-friendly equipment possible.

'The GrainFather,' he said in his email, 'is an all-in-one beer-making machine – a revolution in home brewing that vastly simplifies the beer-making process by allowing you to mash, boil and sparge in one container.' No, me neither.

I read the operating instructions for the sixteenth time. Then I sat down and put my head in my hands.

Three months passed.

*

Great mists engulfed the Richelieu Forest across the road from our bedroom window. Everywhere wood smoke poured from chimneys. Mice came into the house to escape both the cold and the owls that patrolled the vast, clear night skies with electric shrieks. Burt ate the mice. He was a destroyer of all things.

The silence over the countryside was punctuated by occasional shotgun blasts as the locals went out hunting and drinking in the fog (what could possibly go wrong?). They love to hunt here. It's not a pursuit for posh dicks as it is in England. Here, it's a right of the ordinary people, a legacy of the revolution. They hunt to eat. I believe this is at least partly because it takes so long to master the absurdly complicated opening hours of French shops that it's quicker just to get drunk and shoot your future dinner.

Long nights got even longer. The village of Braslou was deserted. The town of Richelieu was deserted. People hibernate during winter over here. David, husband of Mishi, who we bought the house from, an ex-army officer and deep-sea diver, an action man carved out of flint, described the winters to us as 'desperate'. Without entirely agreeing with him, I liked that description. 'Desperate,' I would repeat it to people whenever I got the chance.

We did nothing all winter but chop wood and burn wood. The house was cold. There was no central heating, only the two fires and some weak electric heaters in the bedrooms. By day we huddled around the fires drinking coffee. At night we went to bed in as many pairs of pyjamas as we could fit. It was quite fun at the time, but already I could feel the responsibility of being a father. There was no way we could keep a baby here in these conditions. We'd have to get something done about it before next winter.

In January, we decided we needed to find some signs of humanity and so we piled into the 1999 Renault Mégane and went to the nearby town of Chinon for the day. There was something going on in the town hall, so we thought we'd check it out. If you haven't been to Chinon you're a fool. It's a marvellous place. An enormous fort stretches along a ridge above the town, which tumbles down the hill onto the banks of the Vienne. King John of Robin Hood infamy lived there till he ballsed everything up and had to make a retreat back to England. I had a lot of sympathy for him. Outside the town hall a group of people had gathered. We approached to find they were watching a man leading a pig around with a bit of string. As entertainment goes it was still better than French television.

Inside the town hall it was going crazy. Pumped-up, rich, hostile French people charged from stall to stall staring at what appeared to be rabbit droppings. We'd been in France long enough now not to be surprised at anything. We thought we'd better join in.

'You have to sniff them. I've seen people sniff them,' said Rose.

I picked up a rabbit dropping and sniffed it. It was unbearable. 'I'll take it!' I announced commandingly.

'That will be eighty-seven euros,' said the woman behind the table.

'I won't take it. I refuse to pay more than fifty euros for a rabbit dropping.'

'It's a truffle,' said the woman behind the table.

'No. You're a truffle,' I responded, brilliantly.

A bell rang to signify there was only ten minutes left of the truffle sale. The place went insane. It was Truffle Fever. I may one day make a novelty '70s funk album called *Truffle*

8

Fever. Caught in the moment, we identified the smallest truffle we could find and purchased it for €30 after ensuring it wasn't a rabbit dropping.

We kept the truffle for a month. It sat glowering at me when I opened the fridge – a constant reminder of the day I saw a pig on a string.

As February arrived the mists cleared, exposing skeletal trees. Fields were frostbitten and barren. Log piles dwindled.

I'd been staring at the GrainFather all winter, hoping that beer would suddenly and miraculously come pouring out, but it had produced nothing. *Perhaps it's the wrong season*, I thought. *Maybe it needs pollination from the bees*, I thought. A couple of phone calls to Chris dispelled these theories. On his recommendation I began reading a book called *How to Brew* by Jon Palmer, which covered absolutely every aspect of brewing, but the more I read, the more complicated the whole thing seemed. There was science involved. Enzymes, for God's sake. Chris had not mentioned this to me. Nothing puts one off doing things more than the involvement of enzymes. Also, it turned out there was much more equipment needed than just the GrainFather: malt, hops, yeast, fermenters, siphons, plastic tubs, metal pots, hoses, bottle fillers, bottle caps, refractometers and a bottle-capping machine, just for starters. Over the winter the only home-brewing area where I had achieved any success was in collecting empty bottles. They weren't empty when I bought them of course – they were full of beer. I had spent three months merrily drinking beer after beer from bottles of all shapes and sizes in the name of building up stocks. I'd drunk everything France had to offer. I'd drunk so much beer I'm fairly certain I'd unsettled various international stock exchanges. By February, you couldn't move for empty beer bottles. The place looked like it had been invaded by a rampant glass fungus.

It was 11 February. A depression hung over the house. Burt had chewed through the wire of the electric radiator in the kitchen, making it uninhabitable for large parts of the day. I knew what he was doing. He was trying to shut the house down room by room. I was being haunted by my nan's alarm clock and no brewing had been achieved. Rose had lost all faith in me. She was four months pregnant. That morning I was sitting morosely in front of the fire drinking my third cappuccino. Damien was right about the fire, by the way. It turns out that having a massive hole in the wall makes it burn much better. It's to do with oxygen. It's funny – living in big cities erodes your trust in people. For the first few days after Damien drilled the hole in the wall I was convinced he'd done it as part of a village-wide plan to make our lives so cold and awful that we'd move back to England. Maybe they didn't want the boorish English moving in and ruining their perfect lifestyle with fish-and-chip shops and bottomless cynicism? I was wrong, and with the warmth the fire brought I felt shame that I hadn't trusted Damien. I texted him a few days after he drilled the hole to say thank you. He replied: 'No problem, Tommy. I don't bite.'

Rose came into the kitchen. Her gentle, round pregnancy bump was growing day on day. I rested my coffee on my gentle, round beer bump, which was growing day on day.

'I've been offered an interview for some social-media marketing work,' she announced. 'If I get it I can do it remotely from here. I have to go to London this weekend for an interview.'

'What? Don't get a job. We moved here to avoid jobs. You hate that social-media rubbish. Why don't you just concentrate on your ceramics?'

'Tommy, I'm four months pregnant. We need some money. Face facts. The only money we've made is from me selling a few sculptures and it's not nearly enough for us to live on, let alone bring up a baby with. You still haven't found a publisher and you're never going to brew anything, let alone sell anything. The money has almost run out. We need the income.' She paused. 'All you do is drink beer all day.'

'Hey, don't bring my drinking into it. I'm having to drink double the amount of beer to build up our bottle stocks because you aren't contributing. If anyone isn't pulling their weight, it's you.'

'Of course I'm not contributing – I'm pregnant, you idiot. And what's the point of having all these empty bottles if you don't have anything to put in them? Whenever a door slams it sounds like we're living in a giant glass wind chime. Look, maybe you should get a normal job too?'

'I'm not going back to an office, Rose. No way.'

'Oh, for God's sake. OK, perhaps you could become a freelance graphic designer and work from home?'

I snorted with contempt. 'Have you any idea what a bunch of bell-ends freelance graphic designers are? The cost of hair gel alone would be insurmountable.'

'At least think about it.'

We spent the next couple of days not speaking to each other. There was no way I was going back to what I had been doing before. I had escaped all that. That was the whole point.

I dropped Rose off at Tours airport on the Friday

evening and went back to bed for the weekend. Partly because I had the sort of hangover that only three months of solid drinking can provide and partly because I felt really, really disappointed. I thought I was disappointed with Rose because she hadn't stuck with my plan for us to be artists and brewers and swan around in the sun, eating French cheese and never again having to deal with all the tedious shit that comes with an office job, but I gradually realised that I wasn't disappointed with her. I was disappointed because she was right and I was wrong. I was disappointed because for the first time I was starting to realise what a stupid idea moving to France was. I was about to start a family and I was still arsing about like a teenager. *What am I doing messing around at my age? I should try and get a proper job. There must be businesses round here that need an incompetent graphic designer. I need to be an adult. I need to provide for Rose. I need to provide for our baby . . .*

A fear of risk, responsibility, and a future that was careering out of control overwhelmed me. Rose was right. I needed to get a job. I opened my laptop with the intention of finding the steadiest office job possible when suddenly that feeling of fear triggered a memory. It reminded me of the last time I felt like that, almost exactly a year before. The day I found out I was being made redundant.

I had been fantasising about being made redundant from my job in a corporate London office for quite some time, but when it actually happened, all of a sudden I felt like I was in a dinghy without oars that had been cut loose from the shore and was floating past a sign saying 'Niagara Falls – Now With Added Crocodiles and U-boats'. I'd spent my last fifteen years going to an office, arsing around for the day before heading home, and in exchange a faceless organisation paid a lump sum into my bank account at the end of the month. That was how life worked. As I sat there at my desk with the letter of redundancy in my hand, it didn't feel like such a bad system. Indeed, why would anyone want to give it up? It occurred to me that I had no idea how life worked without a giant faceless organisation keeping me alive.

That was the last time I had experienced a fear of the future, of having to take direct responsibility for my life – and I remember sitting at my desk feeling terrified. But then I looked around at the alternative. I looked around the office at people sitting in meeting rooms pinching their legs to stay awake, and people making small talk through the fug of microwaved M&S soup in the office kitchen, and the sound of their fake laughter, disguised yawns and stories of tragic work nights out made me want to lie on the floor and weep; I looked at the brown, Brillo-pad-textured carpet tiles and the strip lighting and notices telling us to make sure we'd cleaned our plates before putting them in the dishwasher and trite company slogans peeling off the walls, at the sachets of instant coffee and flip charts torn and defaced with meaningless Venn diagrams badly drawn in green marker pen, and hole punches and staple removers and people I really couldn't stand but had to be nice to, and I thought about the same conversations I'd had every day for fifteen years – and I looked back at my redundancy letter and the fear dissipated.

I knew then that getting out of the office was the only way for me to survive. And now, one year later, I knew that going back to an office wasn't an option. I shut my laptop. If I couldn't go back to an office and no one would publish my novel I only had one alternative: to brew. To feed my family I would brew. Beer would save me. Of course it would! It always had!

I strode into the barn with a new sense of determination and, for the first time in my life, I felt like a glorious, hairy, hunter-gathering, body-odoured, fart-noise-appreciating, bison-wrestling, emotion-hating man.

There's something primal about wearing Y-fronts. Something Neanderthal. They provide an intense connection with nature. Historians to this day argue over whether man preceded the Y-front or vice versa. It seemed natural then, in this fervour of testosterone, to strip down to my Y-fronts. I instantly regretted it. It was February after all and I was in our freezing cold barn. I could feel an Arctic wind blowing through the front flap, and my balls shot up so quickly they bounced off my lungs, but at that crucial moment I knew any sort of backward step could be terminal, so I resolved to continue and make my first brew in nothing but my Y-fronts. I reread the GrainFather instructions, put my head in my hands, took my head out of my hands, read the most basic parts from Jon Palmer's book *How to Brew* and I began to plan my brew. As I did so, I realised that if I ignored all the complicated bits about enzymes, the basic procedure for brewing beer was actually fairly straightforward: turn starch from malt into sugar + add hops + ferment sugar with yeast = beer. Granted, if you actually want to make good beer there are an infinite number of variables you have to take into account, from different techniques to ingredients, to timings to equipment to temperatures, but simply making an alcoholic, mud-coloured liquid was, I realised, just about within the outer ranges of my intellectual capabilities, and an alcoholic, mud-coloured liquid sounded absolutely delicious to me.

14

I had a rough idea of the sort of beer I wanted to make. Something close to my favourite beer, Big Job IPA, made by St Austell Brewery in Cornwall. It was 7.4 per cent proof, an American-style IPA made with American hops, which gave the most unusual, exotic flavours.

In the previous few years, the craft brewery phenomenon had erupted. The craft beer movement, if you're not familiar with it, started in the USA in the late 1980s. Previously, the USA had been famous for mass-producing the most appalling, flavourless beer. Their philosophy was the less it tasted of anything, the broader the appeal. Think of mass-produced US beer as the Simply Red of the booze world. A few intrepid Americans led a rebellion against this, setting up small breweries and using hops grown and developed in North America (hops are the ingredients that impart the bitter taste to beer, among other things), hops that hadn't been used to make beer before. I'd say they were the punk rockers of the beer world, except punk music was dire, whereas the beer they were making was spectacular. Perhaps they were the 1980s hair-metal bands of the beer world. This analogy isn't working. The hops that they used proved to be much more powerful than the traditional European hops and the beer they produced was like nothing else. It was the absolute antithesis of the old mass-produced stuff, strong both in alcoholic content and flavour. A revolution was born and swept across the Western world. As momentum gathered, thousands upon thousands of microbreweries sprang up all across North America and Europe. As far as I could tell, the revolution hadn't reached rural France yet.

St Austell Brewery had a list of ingredients for Big Job IPA on their website, so I copied what they had used.

They didn't mention quantities, so that was largely guess-work. I began to grind my malted barley. (Note: if you have that sort of mind, there will be a lot of potential for double entendres in brewing terminology – I won't make those jokes because they are beneath me, but if you feel that terms like 'sparging my grain' are funny, then there's nothing I can do about that. Actually, 'sparging my grain' is definitely funny.) The smell of toasted caramel filled the barn, holding the malted grains in my hand felt wholesome (*Aha*, I thought, *so this is what it feels like to be a Quaker*) and I had the feeling that I was initiating an ancient, magical process. A form of alchemy. When I had ground 6.5 kg of malt, I added it to the heated water in the GrainFather. This is called the mashing stage – the intention is to release the starches from the malt and turn them to sugar. Then I boiled the wort, which is the sugar-rich liquid you are left with once you take away the malt, and added hops, which look and smell suspiciously like skunk weed, to give the beer its bitter flavour. So far everything was going well.

There is a crucial point in the boiling process called the hot break. This is where, as the wort reaches boiling point, a foam made of various proteins in the wort suddenly rises up and if you don't do something about it, by patting it down with a paddle or spraying it with water, it will boil over and the floor, the walls and your naked, Y-front-topped legs will be awash with burning, sticky sugar water. Basically napalm. Jon Palmer warns about this extensively in his book. I was prepared for this. I was on my guard for the hot break. What I was not prepared for was a noise like a punctured bagpipe that came from the garden just as the wort was coming to the boil. I opened the barn doors to see Louis, our other puppy and brother of Burt, vomiting mounds of malt across the lawn with the speed of a Gatling gun, which he was then merrily re-eating, thus continuing his cycle of vomiting. He'd found the pile of hot, wet malt that I'd discarded on the compost heap and promptly eaten his own body weight in it. Without a thought for my own safety, I charged into the garden in my underpants. It was wet and muddy and I slipped into a sort of sliding tackle position, straight through his most recent pile of malt vomit. He ran to a few feet away and once again began his process of vomiting and reconsuming. I got up and charged after him again. Burt, who had been lurking nefariously behind a dustbin, spotted his opportunity, circled round behind me and started eating Louis' previous vomit. I picked Louis up and held his head over the side of my arms as he threw up another powerful jet of grain. I wheeled round on Burt.

'BURT! DESIST!' I screamed, charging at him with Louis under my arm and slipping again, releasing a vomiting puppy into the air. Burt avoided my slide and, delighted, ran off to eat more of Louis' vomit. I ran after him. Louis landed on his back, vomited and promptly ate it. Burt ran behind a tree. Damien strolled past the front gate.

'*Salut*, Tommy!'

'*Salut*, Damien!'

I managed to collar Louis once more and threw him over the gate into the locked front garden before he could eat any more of his own sick. Then I chased Burt round the tree until the fat little bugger ran out of puff and I could carry him into the front garden as well. Finally, with both of them safely locked up, I returned to the barn in my underpants, caked in mud and grain that had been through several digestive cycles to see the last of the foam from the hot break pouring down the side of the GrainFather. My feet stuck to the floor. Everything was covered in a yellow, sticky goo. For a second I thought about giving up on brewing beer and instead earning a living by travelling the local villages and putting on displays where I fired my dogs out of a cannon into a molten volcano, but, using all my willpower, I refocused and by the evening I had cooled what was left of the wort and transferred it to a plastic fermenting barrel. I pitched the yeast (in other words chucked the packet of dry yeast, which would turn the sugar to alcohol, on top of the wort in the fermenter) and as Rose walked through the door I stood proudly in the living room in nothing but my underpants, covered in dried mud and malted vomit grain.

'What the hell happened to you?' she said.

Instinctively I put one foot on the fermenter full of wort as if I was Napoleon Bonaparte.

'Oh, you know. I just brewed some beer. Don't worry about it. How was England?'

BEER NO. 2:
Fat Boy IPA

RECIPE	MISTAKES
6 kg Maris Otter malt	Failure to take a gravity reading post-boil (again)
500 g German pale malt	
30 g Nugget hops at start of boil	Fermentation at wrong temperature for the yeast (again)
20 g Citra hops after 75 minutes	Too many bittering hops
20 g Citra hops after 85 minutes	Eating so much cheese that I turned into cheese
20 g Citra hops post-boil for 10 minutes	Not putting Burt in a box and posting him to Bangkok
15 g American West Coast Ale yeast	

Our house is called La Ruche – the Beehive. It's in the Indre-et-Loire, a region on the south side of the Loire Valley in the centre of France – a countryside of gentle hills quilted in forests and striped with vineyards. Wide, shallow rivers flit between medieval towns while glorious châteaux sit so comfortably on the riverbanks that they look like the scenery has been built around them. I had never heard of the area until we arrived in March 2015 for a two-month stay in a house I had found on the internet. This house, La Ruche, as it turned out. We rented it solely because of the beauty of the decor. It had four-poster beds, an en suite bathroom and two vast fireplaces. Huge oil paintings hung from the walls, there were statues in the loos and a bewildering amount of old trinkets on the mantelpieces, shelves and the two metre by two metre oak coffee table in the living room. We could pretend we were millionaires for a little while. It was fantasy. We didn't for a moment think we'd ever be able to buy it. We thought that even if the area turned out to be a let-down, living in a house like this would be fun. As it turned out, the area wasn't a let-down either.

La Ruche is situated between Richelieu – a walled, moated town built on a grid pattern around two great squares by Cardinal Richelieu in the 1630s – and Braslou, a little village famed for holding a yearly asparagus festival.

It's a Maison de Maître: a tall, symmetrical, dignified old house built with great rectangular blocks of white tuffeau sandstone. Three elegantly carved mansard windows are spaced equally across the black slate roof, with three windows across the first floor and two large windows either side of an imposing front door on the ground floor, flanked by great bushes of rosemary and mint. It has a large front garden separated from the road by an ancient, wisteria-covered, wrought-iron fence. Laurel bushes twenty feet high form an arch over the gate to the road. To the right is another garden – wilder, with a tall pine and some smaller bushes forming an intimate dell and in the corner a thickset, tuffeau-built barn. Another large barn with giant wooden doors is attached to the back of the house. It would have been built to shelter the master's carriage. Behind the house is a drowsy-looking orchard of apple trees and wild cherry trees, some old grape vines running down the right-hand side, half overgrown with brambles, and another great pine in the far left corner. It is bordered on two sides by sunflower fields and at the back by a brambly copse. Over the road is Richelieu Forest, a huge forest full of oaks and pine trees with a sandy floor that runs all the way from the park in Richelieu out into the countryside.

La Ruche sits at the bottom of a ridge that runs like a collar across the back of Richelieu along the road to Braslou. In all, there is nearly 3,500 square metres or just under an acre of land. Not particularly large for rural France, but coming from a one-bed flat in London with the total floor space of a Ford Mondeo, it now felt like we had the planet to ourselves.

The kitchen is enormous – white-and-blue patterned tiling around the walls and even on the dining table. I'd never seen a tiled table before. What next – a wallpapered toilet bowl? A grand fireplace is installed in the left-hand wall, mirroring the fireplace in the living room. Two large dressers sit comfortably against the walls – one white and one sea green to match the rest of the cupboards. Copper pots hang from an iron circle a foot in diameter, which in turn hangs from the ceiling. It's a high ceiling. All the ceilings are high. You could easily have fitted another floor into the house if there weren't such high ceilings. But that is one of the things I love most about it. Despite its size, there are only three bedrooms and that includes the converted attic, but all the rooms are huge. There is space everywhere. When you walk into the house the space fills your lungs and you relax. If the architect who designed my old flat in

London had got his hands on this house he would have partitioned it off, both horizontally and vertically, into studio flats so small that you could only open the oven door if any visitors stood in the garden.

In late February, I went back to England for my brother's fortieth birthday party. Rose stayed at home with the dogs. I hadn't really noticed much difference between the two countries until I went to the toilet in an English service station and I saw an old friend. A friend I hadn't seen in a place like this for a long time. A loo seat.

Long-running feuds can be hard to understand. Families have been known to feud for generations over matters that to the outsider seem barely trivial. Sometimes there are feuds that have gone on for such long time that the participants no longer know why they are feuding and yet they continue, despite neither side benefiting from it. And so I wonder what trivial slight could have started the feud between the French and toilet seats. Bars, restaurants, public toilets, campsites, motorway service stations. You won't find a single toilet seat in any of them and, like the bitterest feuds, it causes both sides to lose out and yet neither will relent.

You're going to reel out the old line about the French only having toilets that are a hole in the floor, but you're wrong. Yes, the French have traditionally lagged behind the British in toilet technology – it was common even ten years ago to find a hole in the floor where the toilet should be, but here's the bit I don't understand: in recent years they've made such advances. They've really made the effort to catch up. Nowadays, almost everywhere you go the hole-in-the-floor toilets have been replaced by proper toilet bowls (consequently the French have noticeably thinner thighs).

Admittedly they still put urinals in the same places as the British would put public telephones. In two of my favourite restaurants in France it's possible to wave to the people working behind the bar whilst taking a pee. Turns out they find that unsettling. Anyway, generally they've gone to the trouble of installing proper loos in cubicles with doors and locks. But this is the thing. They have gone to all the trouble of installing the loos and they have come so close to joining the rest of civilisation and then they haven't bothered putting the loo seats on. There's not a public loo seat in France.

In many public toilets they've actually installed machines that dispense paper loo seats for you to rest on the rim and flush away afterwards. *Just put a proper loo seat on it.* Put a seat on it, for crying out loud. What has the loo seat done to be so roundly shunned by an entire nation? I must ask Damien.

I spent a day or two in London enjoying loo seats. Travelling on the Underground seemed even more absurd than it did when I had lived there a year ago. It was like being canned with flannel-covered chicken legs in a brine of commuter sweat. It reminded me of the moment several years before when I first realised I had to leave London.

It was a classic, grey-on-grey, British November day in 2012. The Tube was damp, cold and busy – people sneezed in each other's hair. I had managed to get a seat for the first time all year after a passive–aggressive standoff with a man in a roll-neck jumper and breath steeped in six-day-old Nescafé. The train slithered and squealed into Oxford Circus station, which was lit by strip lighting so harsh it could peel paint. I watched as the commuters in my carriage who hadn't been lucky enough to get a seat – pallid, exhausted, their faces squashed against the windows – eyed the sea of people awaiting us on the platform, who were

23

coiled and ready to hurl themselves at the opening doors of a Tube train that was already packed so tightly that it was straining at the rivets.

Most of the people waiting on the platform wouldn't be able to get on. They knew that. And yet they knew they had to try. And so the doors slowly opened and it began: one commuter after another hurling themselves from the platform at the mass of bodies in the train like penguins firing themselves out of the water and onto an iceberg to escape a killer whale. Most simply bounced off and back onto the platform, but one or two managed to cling on – a middle-aged, sharp-spectacled, sharp-elbowed woman who was almost certainly a marketing executive and a lofty man in a pinstripe suit – forcing the weaker commuters out of the way, shoving, barking orders, finding space where there was no space, ignoring angry mutters and the odd retaliatory nudge. The doors closed. People shuffled their feet, adjusting to the ever-decreasing space. Annoyance dissipated and a grudging respect for those who had made it remained. There was no sympathy for those who were left behind. And off we trundled to the next station, where this primal battle for survival would be repeated – a battle that occurred every day at every central London Underground station between the hours of 8 and 10 a.m. and 5 and 7 p.m. A battle that I had participated in every weekday for fifteen years. But it wasn't this scene that made me realise I had to leave. Not directly, anyway.

If you get on a packed train in London and yet there is one person sitting down with the seats either side of them free, it is because the person sitting between the free seats is a lunatic. This is a certainty. This is one of the first things one learns when living in London. Indeed, one of the few joys of a London commute is when a situation like this arises and the whole carriage, bar one unsuspecting tourist, knows why there are two free seats available. Astounded by their luck, our tourist pushes past the commuters and sits down, only to find themselves, within seconds, forced to field questions from the person next to them about whether they should interpret the current formation of Jupiter's moons as a sign that they should kill again. A momentary shaft of glee penetrates the carriage before the doors shut like great, squealing misery curtains and everyone returns to avoiding eye contact and grimacing.

But this day in November 2012, something peculiar happened. Much to my surprise, I realised the empty seats were either side of me. I was suddenly aware that I had been narrating the scene I had witnessed on the platform at Oxford Circus in the style of David Attenborough. Out loud. I glanced around the train. A toddler stared at me with a look of pure wonder. Everyone else made an extra-special effort not to make eye contact. I caught my reflection in the window. My hair was still flattened on one side from my bed and projected out in disparate tufts on the other. For the last five years, while I still spent my days in the office, I'd spent my evenings performing stand-up comedy, at first three or four times a week in front of miniscule audiences of bemused hipsters and foreign-exchange students in London, before graduating to low-level gigs in the commuter villages and towns that encircled the capital, which normally meant getting home in the early hours of the morning and even then not being able to sleep because you were still buzzing from the unmatchable feeling of making a room full of people laugh at the stupid things you said or, conversely, you were torturing yourself by endlessly playing over in your head the fact you failed to think of a comeback at the excruciating gig where you were heckled off by a heroin addict in some run-down pub in Brighton. It meant I was getting at best three or four hours sleep a night and now it was taking its toll.

I hadn't bothered to shower. It wasn't shower day. I couldn't remember when 'shower day' had replaced showering every day, but it had. My eyes were dull. For the first time I noticed how sad I looked. It was the expression I had worn for several years, and for the first time I could see it was an expression of unhappiness. I realised that I hadn't really thought about anything that morning until I saw myself in the window. I had got up, eaten breakfast, thrown on the same clothes I always threw on, caught the train – and I hadn't engaged my brain once. And then I realised I hadn't thought about anything the day before. I had gone to work, I had made the same gags that I made every day, I had looked at the internet, I had done some second-rate graphic design and I had come home, all the time without ever really *thinking*. And then I realised it was the same the day before that. In fact, I couldn't remember the last time I'd really thought about anything. And I hadn't really felt anything. I hadn't felt anything for months. I was suddenly aware that at some point in the last few years I had stopped living. And then, for the first time in as long as I could remember, as people on the Tube edged away from me, I had an actual feeling. A feeling that starts deep in your gut and resonates right through your body. A feeling of urgency. A feeling that I had to escape before it was too late. It was an awakening. A last warning.

Now, four years later, I looked with pity at the people on

the train. I don't know, perhaps it was just me who wasn't happy living like that, but I was so pleased I didn't have to any more, and I couldn't wait to get back to France and see Rose. And I couldn't wait to brew more beer.

Burt dropped half a slipper at my feet, looked at me is if to say 'You're a prick' and waddled off. It was the fourth pair of slippers he had eaten in two weeks. I had decided I would try to build bridges with him by training him to fetch my slippers in the morning. I thought it would bring us closer. I had a vision of us loafing in the study, me in a quilted smoking jacket, chuffing on a pipe and sipping brandy while reading about the East India Company in a giant broadsheet, and Burt, my faithful hound, trotting dutifully to my side, slippers delicately balanced in his jaws. So I started to train him by throwing my slippers and giving him a little treat when he brought them back. Burt realised very quickly that I needed my slippers more than he needed a little treat. He began blackmailing me into giving him more and more treats before he would bring the slippers back. Eventually, he decided that he didn't need treats at all; the simple pleasure of whisking my slippers off into the garden in the cold, wet February mornings and chewing them to shreds while I chased after him through the mud in bare feet and pyjamas was by far the most pleasure he could extort. It was a welcome relief when March came and the temperature began to lift.

By the time I had returned from London the cherry trees in the orchard were exploding into blossom. The grass verges on the road that dizzily winds up from Richelieu to Braslou had begun to sprout. Either side of the road the fields were dotted with old red and green tractors. Spring was coming. Farmers were in the fields planting asparagus. I was on the up.

My plastic fermenter full of beer had been bubbling away under the stairs for three weeks, a cloudy reminder of my errors. And as the weeks went by and I read more on the process of brewing, I realised I had made many errors that could have ruined my beer but, despite this, it seemed to be fermenting. At its peak, it was burping out gases through the airlock on top of the fermenter as regularly as a heartbeat. It had a pulse. I had created life. I was God. I tried to strike Burt down with a lightning bolt. It didn't work.

It took much longer for it to ferment than it should have because I had failed to read the instructions on the packet of yeast. There are two types of yeast that are normally used in brewing – lager yeasts and ale yeasts. I was using an ale yeast. Ale yeasts ferment best at around 22–25°C (lager yeasts ferment at 11–14°C). I was keeping my beer at 15°C, so it took an extra week to ferment. But after three weeks it was ready to bottle.

While Rose showed no outward or indeed inward signs of approval, I'm sure she was on some level deeply impressed with my work. Not nearly as impressed as I was, of course. At one point, when trying to explain to Rose the magnitude of my first brew, I almost compared it favourably to giving birth. However, showing foresight and sensitivity that was most out of character, I realised just in time that this was almost certainly the sort of thing that John Wayne Bobbitt had said to his partner before she lopped off his penis and so I bit my tongue. I did *not* want to lose my penis.

I'm not really an achiever. I start things and then move on when they go wrong or they get too complicated. I bail. I don't see things through. I move from one failed enterprise to the next. I use too many sentences to describe the same thing. I had naturally assumed the beer would be spoilt and taste of brine and then I could forget about brewing and we'd have to move back to England in disgrace and Rose would take the baby and leave me for someone who was able to plan further than twelve hours into the future. So when I tasted the beer after the fermentation was finished, I was fully expecting it to cause me to throw up on one of the dogs (who would then eat it), but to my complete surprise it tasted, well, like beer, I suppose. The process wasn't complete yet. It was flat. Once it's fermented, you have to bottle the beer with a little sugar and leave it for a couple of weeks to ferment again in order to get the bubbles, but there was no denying I had actually made beer, and I was baffled. Something was supposed to have gone wrong by now.

We bottled the beer one stormy night in early March, Rose and I. We spent the evening in the corner of the barn, lit in a greenish-white by an electric lantern, which buzzed in and out of life as the water thudded and panged through the holes in the barn roof into carefully placed buckets all around us. Rose filled the bottles from the fermenter and I capped them. We listened to 1980s power ballads while frogs croaked along in the fields behind the barn. To me it was one of the most romantic nights we had ever spent together. I'd imagine Rose would disagree. Two weeks later, twenty-one litres of homemade beer would be ready to try.

We met at work. It wasn't one of those extravagant flings. We didn't scream our undying love from the rooftops. It was something much simpler than that. A quiet romance, but fundamental, tangible and permanent. I sometimes

29

think those people who are always posting pictures of theirs and their partner's feet on a sunset-lit beach are trying to convince themselves it's love. We didn't have to convince ourselves. Once I met Rose, there were no choices to be made.

We were in similar positions, although I was much further down the spiral. Rose was a ceramic artist (she made sculptures from clay, not she was an artist made of clay) with a first from Glasgow School of Art. She'd started taking office jobs as a temporary measure to bring in some money while she established herself, but she soon found she couldn't get out of the cycle of monthly pay cheques and mounting debts. She found herself having to do more and more office work until it took over and she hardly had any time to make things. After a few jobs she ended up at the same place of work as me. I too had taken a temporary office job so that I could save a bit of money while I worked out what I wanted to do, but twelve years later I found myself in the same office job with triple the debts I had started with. I know loads of people who did the same thing.

Rose was in danger of forgetting she was an artist. I had long ago forgotten what I was supposed to be. But together, like prisoners of war, we began to form an escape plan.

The plan rested entirely on both of us being made redundant. That was the only way we could clear our debts and start from the beginning. We knew we had to get out of London, and Rose knew she wanted to work solely on her art. Initially I still had no idea what I wanted to do.

At first we thought about moving down to Cornwall, but the property prices there were nearly as high as London. Then Rose found a cider orchard and cottage for sale in Brittany on the internet. It was less than a quarter of the price of a one-bed London flat. At first, we joked about moving to France to make cider, but the advert remained for several weeks, and we became more and more curious until eventually I phoned up to see if it was still available. It wasn't. It had just been sold, but it felt like we had glimpsed an alternative reality. One that wasn't shit. We decided then that, if redundancy came through, we would move to France.

I had fond memories of France. I spent my childhood summers eating boiled sweets, losing fights with my brother and throwing up in the back of a sweltering Ford Cortina with a boot full of cheese that my father insisted on buying in Calais and that gently warmed and ripened and filled the car with an odour that I would describe as 'arse biscuit of cow' as we continued on an endless drive to a mythical campsite in the South of France while my dad played his *Best of Tina Turner* cassette ad infinitum. Actually, I have no idea why I had fond memories of France, but I did. I'd also recently seen a documentary about TV chef Keith Floyd, in which he seemed to spend all of his time in the garden of his French château drinking the finest red wine under the glow of the Provençal sun to the sound of cicadas and corks popping. 'That could be me!' I thought as I sat in my one foot by one foot living room/kitchen/bathroom in central London and gulped on a bottle of the cheapest beer Tesco Metro had to offer. The next day I read in the papers that Keith Floyd had died of a heart attack. 'That could be me!' I should have thought, but didn't.

We began planning in more detail. We would travel round France for a year. In that time Rose would sell her flat and when we found a nice cottage somewhere in the French countryside we would buy it outright with the money from the sale. We'd use any leftover money to turn a barn or garage into a studio for Rose. We would have chickens, we would grow vegetables and we would leave them in the ground and go and eat steak frites at the local café instead.

There had been talk of redundancies at work for some time now. People were outraged when they heard, but I wasn't that bothered. I reckoned I'd probably been there for nine years or so. I couldn't remember precisely because trying to remember my work career felt like trying to find a wellington boot in a muddy pond, but I thought I'd probably get a decent pay out to tide me over for a month or two while I found another job I didn't really want to do. But the incident on the Tube train had awoken something in me and so I decided to look into how much I would get if I was made redundant. I was shocked. It turned out that my organisation had a rather generous redundancy scheme. Not only that – I hadn't been there for nine years. I had been there for twelve years. Somewhere within the big muddy pond I'd managed to lose three years of my life. The good news was those extra three years meant a much bigger payout than I had anticipated. Indeed, if they made me redundant I would get enough money to pay off all my credit cards and loans with money to spare. I could escape.

Wonderfully, the rumours of a restructure and consequently a number of redundancies proved to be true. Rose was offered redundancy and took it immediately. My situation was more complicated. There was one offer of redundancy for my department, which would have been OK if it was just me that wanted it, but unfortunately a work colleague who did a similar job to me wanted to take redundancy as well. They had to make a decision between the two of us. It was deeply unfair – HR work on the assumption that redundancy is a bad thing and people would prefer to keep their job, so to decide whether my colleague or I was given redundancy they scored us based on our performances up until this point, with the lesser performer being given the boot. This meant that the person who had worked harder, contributed more and didn't spend forty-five minutes a day on the loo learning French would effectively be punished for their good behaviour by missing out on redundancy. It wasn't a contest. My colleague was diligent, hard-working, creative and punctual. I had been disciplined several times for sleeping under my desk and twice for being caught impersonating the chief executive. Once by the chief executive. I remember my second dressing-down clearly.

'Tommy, the chief executive has complained that you are impersonating him again,' said my long-suffering boss, Emma.

'Not guilty.'

'You've got a sign on your desk saying "Tommy Barnes – Chief Executive".'

'Ah . . . But chief executive of what? That's the real question, isn't it? Chief executive of *what*?'

'That's not the question at all. Please put the sign away.'

This time it was different. This time when she called me over to the seating area in the kitchen she had a smile on her face.

'Tommy, you are being made redundant. Congratulations! Now, be honest,' – she winked – 'have you been deliberately performing incompetently to get redundancy? It's OK. It was obvious you weren't happy here. You needed a change.'

'Oh. Yes. Right. Sorry about that,' I lied, slightly taken aback. It hadn't occurred to me that I could influence my chances of being made redundant. I simply wasn't very good at my job. I probably would have been OK if I'd tried, but I couldn't take work seriously. That had always been my problem. The meetings. The jargon people used. I watched some people come into the office and shoot up the ranks. They said all the right things, they made suggestions in meetings instead of sketching fellow office members as centaurs, they actually knew what it was our organisation did, whereas I still saw work as a stopgap before I went to do something else that I was actually interested in. There was no reason to take it seriously because I wasn't there going to be there for long. It was just a stopgap. A twelve-year stopgap.

'Your final day will be 27 February. I must say, I'm really excited for you and Rose. There's no way I'd be brave enough to give up the security of my job and a regular salary and move to France unless I had a rock-solid plan to make a living over there like you do. What's the plan again?'

'Well, it's really very simple, Emma. Rose is going to be a famous artist and I'm going to write a comedy/crime thriller bestseller and brew internationally renowned beer and sell it to the French.'

Emma broke into a fit of coughing. I thought I was going to have to perform the Heimlich manoeuvre. Luckily, she recovered before I could. I'd only performed the Heimlich manoeuvre once before, and that was on a vicar choking on a sausage roll at a village fête. I say Heimlich manoeu-vre – I don't actually know how to perform the Heimlich manoeuvre, so I punched him in the stomach repeatedly until he threw up into the tombola.

'Oh. Good luck with that,' said Emma. 'Send us a postcard.'

Charlus stared at me. A large, rugged man in his early twenties with the presence of a storm cloud. He stood square on, no more than a metre away. I didn't know where to look. A couple of the other lads giggled in the corner. One of them said in French, 'Look at him stare!'

I glanced at my football boots and round the modern changing room, which was much better than the ones in England, doing my best to avoid eye contact, wondering when Charlus was going to hit me in the face. After several seconds I plucked up the courage to look back at him. It was then I saw it wasn't an aggressive stare. It was an inquisitive stare.

The French like to stare. I had forgotten that. And why not? There's nothing wrong with looking at each other. It was common in Richelieu, the local town, for someone to stare at you as you walked all the way from one end of the street to the other. It wasn't aggressive; they just wanted you to say hello to them. In England if you stare at someone it is inexplicably viewed as an act of war – one must immediately find a car park in which to thump each other – but in France it's perfectly OK to stare while you work out what on earth a tubby, 38-year-old Englishman with a large, unkempt beard is doing in the changing rooms of your local football club, ASJ Braslou.

The reason, as it happened, was that on my trip back to the UK for my brother's fortieth birthday, people had generally met me with the phrase, 'You look well.' They meant, 'Jesus, you are one fat, fat fuck.' The constant boozing and all the delicious French cheeses I had consumed over winter had combined to have a profound effect on my waistline and I had resolved to do something about it when I got back to France by joining the village football team. Not only that, one of the downsides to moving to a new country is you leave all your friends and family behind. Now, I have always been quite an independent person, and by that I mean not very popular, but no matter how comfortable you are with your own company, one soon realises one needs to socialise. One needs to be part of a group.

'You live here now?' said Charlus. I could barely understand his French. It was thick, fast and heavily accented.

'Yes,' I said.

'You have a woman?'

'Um. Yes.'

'She is French?'

'No, English.'

Charlus seemed relieved that I hadn't come over to steal his women. He stared at me for a moment longer and then turned around and began getting changed.

As I walked out to the pitch I felt someone put their arm around me.

'Welcome to the countryside!' said Charlus, with a big grin, in the same way that St Peter might welcome you through the Pearly Gates. I liked Charlus.

I hadn't played football for six years. Before the training session I remembered myself as a player with skill and class but who lacked aggression and a winning instinct. As it turned out, my memories were 50 per cent correct.

I chugged around artlessly for an hour and a half, swinging my limbs vainly in the direction of footballs that I could just about make out through sheets of sweat. Everything was exhausted. My teammates enjoyed the spectacle a great deal. I was twenty years older than most of them. To an unknowing onlooker it must have looked like a group of young men were baiting Pavarotti.

They realised quite early on that I wasn't the star player who was going to transform their season. In fact they realised that almost immediately I arrived, when I revealed my cheese-crafted body in the changing rooms before we'd got anywhere near the football pitch, so rather than focusing on improving me as a footballer, they took it upon themselves to teach me to swear properly in French. They were just like English footballers really. They were loud, crude, and most of all they were very funny. The humour revolved almost entirely around bodily functions, but they were funny.

The big difference between ASJ Braslou and English teams I had played for was that after the training (which finished at 10 p.m.) everyone went into the Braslou clubhouse, where they handed out beers and crisps – so far so normal. However, much to my astonishment, after about twenty minutes they all sat down either side of long trestle tables and had a cooked meal with a glass of red wine. It was actually civilised. Most conversations were still punctuated by musical farts, but still, it was civilised. It was like eating with a family. I couldn't understand what most of them said – they were farmers and tradesmen who had thick accents and talked in slang – but they were kind to me, the atmosphere was warm and jovial and they went out of their way to make me feel welcome. We were starting to be accepted into the village.

I talk about the people of Braslou as if they are some kind of lost Amazonian tribe. They're not, as far as I know. I should check that. But you can get from our house in Braslou to London in two and a half hours, door to door.

It's not exactly the other side of the world. Braslousians are good, generous, normal people. However, there are cultural differences and language barriers and so it was a relief that I was feeling like I was starting to belong.

When I heard the hiss as the cap came off, I was overcome with pride. Pride that I had managed to do something that I never thought would be possible. It reminded me of the first time I had sex, both the feeling and the duration. I tasted it. It wasn't bad! It was fizzy, it was alcoholic, and it tasted of beer. The Citra hops were coming through. I was a genius!

'It's too bitter,' said Damien. 'And it has a funny smell.'

For a moment I was deeply hurt. I wanted to tell Damien that the French knew nothing about beer and they should stick to topless sunbathing and building shit cars, but I gathered myself and tasted it again. He was right. I knew he was right. Dammit.

'It's not bad, though. It's very good for a first go,' added Damien, standing by the door of the kitchen. Damien very rarely sat down in our kitchen. I don't know if he just didn't like sitting down or if it was the etiquette in France to ask someone to sit down in your kitchen, otherwise they would loiter. I was constantly worried about French etiquette.

He was right again. It wasn't perfect, but it was drinkable and it wasn't realistic to aim for much more than that with one's first brew. Pride and elation returned. For a moment the whole brewery idea didn't seem entirely ludicrous. It was mostly ludicrous, yes, but not impossible.

'Have you thought about brewing blonde beer. People round here like blonde beer,' said Damien.

'Yeah. I will brew a blonde beer one day. No probs.' I said. I had no intention of brewing blonde beer. The craft beer revolution was built on IPAs, not blonde beer. People round here may not realise they liked IPAs, but they would get it eventually.

By now, Damien and Celia had become our heroes. Whenever we walked past their home (a lovely old farm house situated on the edge of the forest with horses in paddocks and a tower that Damien had built himself – he was a stonemason – he'd built a tower!), their daughter Colleen, a sort of a West End musical combined with the mischief of Groucho Marx and squashed into the body of a six-year-old, would stick her head out of the window and shout, 'Coo coo!' and they would invite us in for a drink. They invited us to dinner parties and introduced us to their friends despite our appalling French, they translated voice-mail messages that we couldn't understand because of our appalling French and they told us we didn't have appalling French. At least that's what I think they said. They may have said we do have appalling French. What the French actually say to us is so often a grey area. They made sure we didn't get ripped off by the local tradesmen – Damien had lived in the area all his life and knew them all – and so, while to them we were just an awkward English couple who had inexplicably moved to their village and were incompetent in all the ways of the countryside, unbeknownst to them they were our new best friends. We had to play it cool and not tell them they were our best friends, but they were. I'm not even sure they liked us. I mean, we had nothing to offer them, but they were the kind of people who would help you out, regardless of whether they thought you were a couple of fools from England who didn't know their own arses. They were good people. Our secret best friends. It was only natural that I should invite them over for the first tasting. Celia couldn't drink of course. By now, rather marvellously, she was pregnant too. She was due three months after us. It was great for Rose to have someone else with whom to express mild disapproval of Damien and me. We were tasting my beer on a Saturday morning after all.

I held my bottle of beer up to the light and marvelled at it. The first evidence of people making beer was 8,000 years ago. Come to think of it, I think they were still selling it in my old student union. But I was a beer maker now. I was part of an 8,000-year-old tradition. I was a mystic. A village elder. I had arrived.

'To control nature is to control one's destiny, says I,' I said.

'Says I?' said Rose.

'Yes. Says I.'

'Why are you talking like a pirate?'

'Here, Damien, take some bottles and give them to your friends. It would be interesting to know if the people round here will like this style of beer. It's nothing like the beer they brew round here.'

'Says he.'

'Quiet.'

BEER NO. 3:
Chicken-Flasher IPA

RECIPE	MISTAKES
6 kg Maris Otter malt	Not oxygenating the wort
500 g German Wheat malt	Incorrect amount of sugar for carbonation
20 g Nugget hops at start of boil	Impersonating a mobster
20 g Citra hops after 75 minutes	Trying to pay tax
20 g Citra hops after 85 minutes	
20 g Citra hops post-boil for 10 minutes	
15 g lager yeast	

It was late March. Winter's frosty grip was loosening and the people of France began to emerge from their houses. In the fields all around us asparagus grew in long strips covered by plastic.

Burt had taken to eating the solar lamps in our garden. One morning I found the stems of several lights piled up on the lawn like chewed ribs. He was not a fan of renewable energy, proof of what I already suspected: he was here to destroy the world.

I brewed my second batch of beer in much the same way as the first, but without the unnecessary discomfort of wearing only Y-fronts. I made sure to dispose of the used malt straight in the bin so Louis couldn't use it as some sort of full-body irrigation therapy. There's a stage of the brew process called the boil, after you've got all the sugars out of the malt and discarded it, where you boil the remaining liquid for normally an hour or so to get rid of any unwanted bacteria that might ruin it. This is also the stage where you add hops to flavour the beer. Depending on when you add the hops during the boil, they do different things. Adding hops at the start of the boil gives the beer its bitterness. The more you add, the more bitter it becomes. Adding hops later in the boil, with ten or five minutes to go, imparts the other hop flavours. Depending on what type of hop you use, these could be anything from tropical fruit to floral to grassy and herbal. After Damien's criticism that it was too bitter, this time I added fewer bittering hops at the start of the boil and more hops at the end of the boil to reduce the bitterness and give it more of the exotic fruit flavours that the Citra hop can impart.

A plan was starting to form. It wasn't a plan I would ever really carry out, because it required dedication and a degree of skill; it was more of a fantasy, really. I would invest in another fermenter or two, which meant I could now have several beers fermenting at the same time. I could focus one fermenter on perfecting a staple beer, the beer that I would sell regularly – a strong, American-style IPA, like my favourite beer, Big Job, and I would use the other fermenter to experiment with other styles of beer. Once I had perfected my staple beer I would somehow invest in a professional microbrewery and start selling it at the local markets and farm shops. Nobody in the area was making beer like mine. In England now there was a microbrewery in every town, making IPAs with hops from around the world, but this trend hadn't reached rural France. This, I decided, meant one of two things. Either the market was primed for a brewery like mine and I would clean up, or, equally as likely, the French, who are notoriously picky in their tastes, had no interest in this style of beer and I would fail. I resolved to find out. To establish a brewery and actually start bringing in some money would take time, though, and, as the image of my nan's wood-panelled alarm clock – which since the day I'd found out we were having a baby appeared every time I closed my eyes, counting down to some terrible unknown – reminded me, this was time I did not have. The GrainFather was fine for home brewing, but, due to economies of scale, to brew enough beer to sell at a profit I would need bigger, more professional equipment. Expensive equipment. No. Rose was right. I would need to get some kind of part-time job to bring in more money. Not office work, though.

Nick and Claire were barbecuing chicken. We had been introduced to them by our friends Ali and David, who lived in Richelieu and knew everyone. Both couples were expats. The good sort, though.

Some expats move to France and make a great effort to learn the language and immerse themselves in French culture. Others don't learn any more French than they need to order a beer. They're the ones who only mix with other British people. They organise fish-and-chip nights, they are outraged when shop staff don't speak English and, without a hint of irony, they sit outside the PMU café in Richelieu bemoaning families from Bangladesh that move to England and don't integrate. Damien doesn't like expats who don't try to learn French. He says it shows a lack of respect to move to France and not learn French. I think he's right. I remember going to a dinner party when we had first arrived and listening to some absolute bore banging on about how integration wasn't important. His mum was an Italian immigrant in America or somewhere and she hadn't integrated at all and they were all fine. I wanted to say, 'You're not fine, you're a gargantuan douche box,' but I'm terrified of confrontation, so I left it. But I mean, if no one integrates, if everyone stays in their little groups, then everyone is poorer for it. You learn a lot from other cultures, you make new friends, and cultures are ingrained in the earth that you stand on. They develop from their environment. If you want to live in that environment, of course you should join in. It's not like people are asking you to disown your own culture. You add to it.

There's a reasonable-sized expat community in our area. Not as big as the ones in Brittany and the Dordogne, where there are so many Brits that some villages have British mayors, but there are a significant number of Brits. Most of them are retired. All of them live in old houses that they have renovated. The French have mixed feelings about them. Damien was weary of expats buying houses and not living there all the year round, meaning that villages were half empty when it wasn't high season, but the way I see it, half these houses would have fallen into ruin if they hadn't been bought by the Barrys and Deborahs from the Home Counties and restored.

Nick and Claire weren't your typical expats. They

weren't retired, they were in their early forties and used to work in finance in the City, but they had packed it in, like us, and now lived all year round in a beautiful old village on top of a hill called Faye-la-Vineuse, about fifteen minutes from Braslou. They made their money gardening for people with second homes in France. They spent their days in the sun and their nights barbecuing and drinking local wine. It seemed like a great way to make a living. While Nick prepared the barbecue, I bored him with my financial predicament.

'I've got so much work that I could pass you some of my clients if gardening is something you're interested in. There are lots of elderly expats and people with holiday homes who need their lawns mowing and their hedges trimming when they are back in England,' said Nick as he shoved a beer can up the chicken's arse and placed it upright on the barbecue. For a moment it looked like it was flashing me until he closed the lid on the barbecue to let it cook.

'You know what, Nick? I think I might be interested in that.' I mean, how hard could gardening be? Only that morning I had watched one of our neighbours, Monsieur Richard, driving an enormous sit-on lawnmower replete with beer holder round his garden in the sunshine. Never had I seen anyone so satisfied. He rode around like he was Henry VIII, so I thought to myself, *Yes! Gardening! It's basically just suntanning on the move.*

I could see immediately that Rose, who'd been listening in to the converstation, was delighted at the thought of me actually doing some work. I imagined myself coming back from a day of lawnmowing – tanned, athletic and a foot taller, to a proud girlfriend, a bottle of wine on the garden table and a delicious meal that veered in my mind between a ham and cheese sandwich and stew, and ended up a stew sandwich.

'OK. I'll do it. I will become a gardener. Stew sandwiches,' I said.

'Stew sandwiches?' said Rose.

'Just the bit about becoming a gardener,' I said. 'Ignore the other bit.'

> Bonjour Monsieur Barnes,
> We invite you for a meeting to discuss your plans to start a brewery and set up a gardening business on 1 April.
> Cordialement
> Chambre de Commerce, Tours

I emailed the Chambre de Commerce in mid-March, the organisation that I was told I needed to register with to get a tax status, outlining my plans for a brewery and gardening. I wanted to become a *micro entrepreneur* – the most simple tax status. They replied a week later inviting me in for a meeting. *Brilliant!* I thought. *They will talk me through the registration process and any other regulations I might need to comply with . . . I'd better wear my Goodfellas jacket.* My Goodfellas jacket is a Prince of Wales checked jacket that is very similar to a jacket one of the gangsters in *Goodfellas* is wearing when he's found hanging on a meat hook in an industrial freezer. It's a nice jacket. I only use it for special occasions, and when I do, I avoid industrial freezers.

The meeting was scheduled for a few weeks later, but I wasn't too worried. I had been warned that France was incredibly bureaucratic, but if that meant waiting a few weeks then it wasn't so bad.

46

April Fools' day, 1 April. The day of the meeting. For the previous two weeks I had been preparing myself for this. I expected to walk out of there a bona fide beer maker, ratified by every law in the land. It was the start of something big. I would be able to look back on this day as the moment I became a success. I dressed up as smartly as I could (Goodfellas jacket), gathered all my documents into my folder, as well as my crib sheet of important questions, which I had translated into French. I drove an hour to Tours, the nearest city to us, where all the local administration seems to be done, through vineyards and across the rivers of the Indre and the Vienne to the banks of the Loire where Tours sits, and by 9 a.m. I was being ushered into an office in the Chambre de Commerce by a tall, serious young man.

'*Bonjour* Monsieur Barnes. Thank you for coming to see us today. I understand you want to start a brewery.' He spoke French very slowly, aware that I was a moron. I immediately warmed to his perceptiveness.

'Yes, that is correct.'

'OK. You have come to the wrong place. You need to go to the Chambre de Métiers.'

'Oh, right. It's just I emailed you with the details . . .'

'Is there anything else I can help you with?'

'Right. Well, I was thinking of doing some part-time gardening while I establish the brewery. I think that was on the email as well?'

'Ah yes, gardening. Good idea.' He consulted his computer. 'I'm afraid you have come to the wrong place. You need to go to the Chambre d'Agriculture.' He showed me to the door. 'Thank you for coming. I am glad to be of help.'

'OK. Is this some kind of April Fools . . .?'

'No. Goodbye.'

As I walked back to my car in a state of bewilderment, I wondered how many other offices in Tours were entirely dedicated to telling people they had come to the wrong place. I guessed about 40 per cent.

I got home and immediately phoned the Chambre de Métiers.

'In order to register with us, you must first come to an introductory workshop. The next one is on 3 June.'

'But that's two months away! And after that I can start?'

'No, after that you must do a week-long management course.'

'In June?'

'Hold on, I will check. No, the next management course is August.'

My nan's alarm clock sprung into view. The numbers had turned red and were flashing. The baby was due at the end of June. There was no way I could wait until August before I started selling beer. There was only one thing for it: I was going to have to start selling beer on the black market. Not only that, and perhaps even more daringly, I was going to have to do some illegal gardening. *Holy shit*, I thought to myself, the thrill of danger causing my knees to knock together, *I'm Errol bloody Flynn.*

BEER NO. 4:

The Worst Fence in Braslou Black IPA

RECIPE	MISTAKES
Malts	Bottles not cleaned properly
5.1 kg Maris Otter	Gardening
300 g Belgian pale malt	Drinking and gardening
300 g Chocolate malt	
300 g Carafa	
Hops	
10 g Nugget	
100 g Citra	
Yeast	
Mangrove Jack West Coast	

Looking back, there's not a finer sight in the world than a cast-iron table, lit fleetingly by a whimsical, early summer sun, spitting petals into the air like great plumes of champagne fizz as it is dragged at great pace through a flower bed by a chronically overweight hound. At the time, however, I lost my shit.

'BURT! FOR GOD'S SAKE, DESIST!' I shouted over the top of the roaring ride-on lawnmower engine as he plundered his way through the Johnsons' garden, wreaking mayhem and destruction at every turn. The Johnsons were particularly particular about their garden.

There are several great philosophical questions that have troubled humanity from the outset and I fear may never be truly answered. However, I am pleased to announce that as I watched Burt over my shoulder, hurtling towards the horizon with cast-iron table in tow, ploughing a ragged furrow through immaculately kept lawns and only coming to a stop when the table became anchored in a hedge, I accidentally answered one of them. The question of whether a ride-on lawnmower can knock over a tree. Yes, people. If the driver is sufficiently distracted by a fat, satanic dog, yes it can. While staring in amazement at Burt over my shoulder, I hadn't realised that the direction of my ride-on lawnmower had altered and when I looked back I found I was on a collision course with a little fruit tree. Before I could work out where the damned brake pedal was, there was a terrible creaking and I had pushed over the young apple tree and mowed it to death.

This was the culmination of a disastrous micro-career in gardening. I had hacked, slashed and burnt my way through a variety of previously well-maintained lawns. I accidentally strimmed Roger's orchids. I chopped Neil and Sally's hedge into some kind of surrealist vision of Hades. Sarah and Andrew had warned me their ride-on lawnmower didn't turn left. They were wrong. It did turn left, just not when you wanted it to. Consequently, I crashed it into their barn. I used too much weedkiller on Julie and Ronald's garden and turned it into the surface of Mars. I accidentally threw a rancid rabbit corpse at one of Barry's neighbours. You see, there are two types of gardener: those who giveth life and those who taketh it away, and it turns out I was a taker. A destroyer of all things. I had more in common with Burt than I realised.

I had started taking Burt gardening with me in another attempt to form some kind of a bond. Burt was in no mood to form a bond. He soon developed a ploy in which he would lay a carefully placed poo in the path of my lawn-mower and watch with glee as I ran it over, scattering said poo all over my lower legs. I would have to spend the rest of the morning pushing the mower with one hand and holding my nose with the other.

The incident of the cast-iron table wasn't really his fault, however. When I arrived to mow the Johnsons' lawn, I had tied his lead to the table so he wouldn't be able to poo in my path and then I had filled his water bowl with the only water I could find, Perrier. Burt had never tried fizzy water before. He wasn't aware of its existence. The bubbles in the water were such a shock to his world view that they caused him to embark on a rampage, table in tow. No normal dog would have been able to drag that table, but Burt had weight on his side.

Interestingly, it wasn't until after I knocked over the tree that I started drinking at work. I wasn't downing bottles of whisky on the job or anything like that. I just mean I started taking the odd bottle of beer for the ride-on lawnmowers. They have beer holders, for God's sake! It was clear they were designed to be driven with beer, so what was I supposed to do? Leave the beer holders un-beered?

I was brought up in a drinking culture. From the age of about fourteen onwards the whole point of anything was to get as drunk as you possibly could. When we were old enough to start going out and hiding at the back of pubs, we would meet up at the station, buying four-packs of Stella Artois, drinking them on the train to the next town, then pub-crawling our way through four or five pubs until we got to the pub in the town centre where we were meeting our friends, and only then would the night and the proper drinking begin. This is what teenagers in shitty provincial towns did when I was young.

I don't wake up in the morning desperate to get drunk. I don't hide my drinking from people and I can go without if I have to. I'm not dependent on booze. Interestingly, I do wake up in the morning desperate for croissants. And I do hide my croissant-eating from others. Sometimes I have two or three a day. My croissant habit has affected my social life. I turn up to dinner parties covered in crumbs and people won't look me in the eye. I hide croissants round the house. It may be that I have a croissant problem. The day Damien told me you could get them delivered directly to your door still ranks as one of the greatest days of my life. Rose is on to me, though. She has banned me from having croissants delivered more than twice a week.

Gardening is difficult. That's what I was talking about. Don't let anyone tell you gardening isn't difficult. I mean, it wasn't all bad. If it was a nice day and you just had to sit on a ride-on lawnmower and drink beer, it could be wonderful. I loved doing Julie and Ronald's garden on a sunny day. Their neighbours were called Gaston and Françoise and they were French farmers in their late eighties. I don't know what the average life expectancy round here is, but it must be higher than normal. Nearly every farmer seems to be in their eighties and nineties, and they are all out driving tractors and tending their crops and womanising (I should think).

Gaston loved to chat. Whenever I cut Julie and Ronald's grass in the morning, he would putter over from his farm on his little old tractor and invite me in for a glass of rosé, which he poured from big unmarked plastic bottles. 'For the strength,' he would say. His wife, Françoise, would hobble in. She wouldn't normally have a drink unless I had brought some beer.

'You want a drink, Françoise?'

'Of course not. It's eleven in the morning!' Françoise would exclaim.

'It's his homemade beer.'

'Oh, beer! Why didn't you say?' Then we'd sit around the table shooting the shit, none of us really understanding each other particularly well, but getting along. After an hour or so I'd roll out of their kitchen and onto a ride-on lawnmower and merrily zigzag my way through Julie and Ronald's orchard, crashing into trees in a state of utter bliss.

A lot of the time it wasn't like that, though. The first half of the year had been unusually wet and cold, which meant I would spend half the day on my hands and knees pulling clogs of grass out of the bottom of jammed lawnmowers.

The second half of the year became excruciatingly hot, so hot that you'd have to try and get the work done before 3 p.m. because from then on the temperatures were in the high thirties. The damp in the first few months had created an ideal environment for a mosquito/horsefly orgy, and so when the sun finally came out a great swarm of mosquitoes and horseflies came with it. Hedge trimming was agony on the shoulders. Weedkiller smelt of perfumed death. People, unsurprisingly, employed me to do the jobs they didn't want to do. The shit jobs. The jobs where you had to balance on top of a wobbly ladder fifteen foot in the air and wave a bladed power tool around. Gardening was killing me, but I had no alternative. My respect for Nick and Claire had quadrupled by the end of the summer – and bear in mind I had quite a lot of respect for them in the first place. You would have too, if you'd witnessed the vigour with which Nick jammed beer cans up chickens' bums.

I met Xavier at a *fête de la bière* (beer festival) in a village just to the east of the city of Tours towards the end of April. My mum had found an advert for the beer festival in our local paper when she came over to stay. I don't know why she was looking for adverts for beer festivals. It's her prerogative. One needs to keep oneself occupied when one is retired.

On the whole, French fêtes were much better than English ones. In my experience, any festival you go to in Britain is now solely concerned with generating maximum profit, but the French, in a move that will strike British events organisers as utterly baffling, still put the emphasis on actually having a good time. For instance, last year, while we were staying in a village called Chantelle in the Auvergne, a region in central France, we went to the village's annual *Fête de la Musique*. It was unlike any music festival I'd been to in England. It was free, the beer was cheap, you could see the stage and – this was the best bit – whereas events in Britain tend to be segregated by age (a British teenager would sooner throttle themselves to death than attend a social gathering with their family), at this fête everyone was there: teenagers, young children, parents and really, really old people in wheelchairs. Everyone was mixing together, chatting, drinking a sort of grapefruit and white wine punch (which is much nicer than it sounds), having fun and dancing to what was one of the dirtiest, loudest heavy metal bands I have ever encountered. I shit you not. They were heavy. Don't get me wrong: this band were good. Not enough spandex and giant hair and 1980s rock for my particular tastes, but they were still good. But man, were they heavy.

At the climax of the event, as elderly women chatted to each other over dessert, the singer sang a song that was specifically about her backside while the guitarist wailed on his guitar and a group of primary-school children gleefully spun each other round at the front of the stage. Every now and then the singer would hold her microphone out towards the crowd and the children would, as one, shout back, 'ARSE!' It was brilliant. If I had any criticism of the gig at all, it's that I was the only one throwing glasses of urine at the stage (I didn't).

That was the Auvergne, though. While the intention is always good, French fêtes can be hit and miss. I remember going to one *Fête de la Musique* in a village in Burgundy a few years ago, where we, along with some bemused local farmers, endured an outrageously pretentious band from Paris playing a three-hour rock opera that was somewhere between a Meatloaf video and a primary-school nativity play. Consequently, I had no idea what this *fête de la bière* would be like. Ideally it would be an opportunity to meet other brewers in the area and to drink lots of delicious beer, but it was over an hour each way and for all I knew it could potentially be a complete waste of time. My friend David Kimber Bates, who lives in Richelieu, agreed to come with me. He was a good companion because, in his own words, 'I've been to loads of French fêtes. You never know what the mad fuckers are going to do.' At least he was prepared.

When we arrived, the signs were not good. As we parked up in the village just east of Tours and got out of the car, we could hear early '90s ragga blasting at an outrageous volume from the direction of the beer festival. We approached cautiously. The fête was on some recreational ground at the edge of the village. A DJ booth stood alone in the field, manned by an enthusiastic young woman who screamed jubilantly over the music words to the effect of 'Are you having a good time?' She wasn't at all interested in the answer. As well as this, dreadlocked men, bare-chested except for leather waistcoats, roamed the field carrying ancient musical instruments. There was a large food tent about thirty yards from the DJ booth in which families desperately huddled, fathers peering through the plastic windows, trying to decide when it would be safe to herd their family to the car park. Opposite was a long, open-sided beer tent patronised by a few hardy drinking pros. We headed straight past the shouty woman playing ragga music and the bare-chested musicians to the beer tent and leant against the bar, bewildered.

'BAT SHIT!' shouted David over the chorus of 'Boombastic'.

'YES. SORRY. I THOUGHT THERE MIGHT ACTUALLY BE SOME LOCAL BEER MAKERS HERE. THIS WASN'T WHAT I HAD ENVISAGED. I'M NOT REALLY SURE WHO THIS IS AIMED AT.'

A middle-aged man in tight denim shorts began gyrating next to the DJ booth.

'HIM,' shouted David. 'JUST HIM.'

Conversation was near on impossible. The beer was local, at least. We had a drink and turned to go.

'WHAT'S THAT OVER THERE?' shouted David,

pointing behind the beer tent. About fifty yards away, through trees and over rubble-strewn waste ground we could see what looked like some kind of stall. We began to make our way through the rubble. There were more stalls. Four in total, in a line. There was no one visiting them because they were almost impossible to spot from the main fête, but, sure enough, they were beer stalls. The beer festival organisers had hidden the beer festival.

And there was Xavier standing behind his stall. Tall, heavy stubble, a weariness that comes with having seen it all and not being particularly bothered about any of it, a face that was perfectly suited to chewing tobacco, Xavier looked like a character from a western. Not the hero, or even the main baddy, but one of the other dudes. Secondary baddy, perhaps. One without a speaking role. We introduced ourselves. I told Xavier that I was an aspiring brewer. It soon became apparent that he was a lovely man. He made mostly Belgian-influenced beers, Tripels, which are very strong abbey beers and blondes in the style of Leffe.

Xavier wrote down places where I could buy local malt, websites where I could buy equipment and gave me free beer. He also invited me to come and see his brewery In Orléans. In return I gave him two bottles of my third brew – a black IPA. It's a sort of a cross between a stout and an IPA. Pedants will tell you that there's no such thing as a black IPA, as the 'P' stands for 'pale'. But I mean, I really can't even— I mean, who even has the energy to give a shit about that? One of my favourite beers is a black IPA called Conqueror, made by Windsor and Eton Brewery. It has liquorice and coffee flavours but then a wonderful, perfectly balanced hit of citrusy hops to finish. My black IPA didn't have much of a hop finish. I hadn't used enough flavouring hops. In fact, I realised I hadn't been using enough flavouring hops in any of my beers up till now. My black IPA was OK. Interestingly, It didn't have that slightly astringent taste that my normal IPAs seemed to have. It was inoffensive, but it wasn't much of a beer, really. I prayed that Xavier wouldn't try it until I had left.

After chatting and drinking with Xavier for half an hour or so, we went to the rest of the stalls. All the brewers were very kind and generous. I bought lots of beer. The beer was excellent, but, on the whole, it was traditional French beer. Nobody at the fête was making American IPAs. I saw this as a positive. American-style IPAs would still be new to my customers. We chatted with brewers for a little while, then, as the ragga music grew louder, we got out of there as fast as we could.

The countryside in May and June was like a slow-motion fireworks display. Dazzling fields of rape exploded out of the springtime from nowhere, and overnight, everywhere you looked was a startling yellow stretching to the horizon. After several weeks it began to fade back to green until suddenly there was another explosion, this time sunflowers saturating almost every field in a warm yellowy orange. Summer had arrived.

By the start of May Rose was eight months pregnant. I often hear men talk about how pregnancy hormones (technical term) sent their partner homicidal for nine months. Hormonicidal. I don't know. But I didn't notice that with Rose. She was really happy. I've never seen anyone so happy. And it made me feel terribly guilty. I was pretending that I had everything covered, that I was earning lots of money gardening and by the end of the year I would have a flourishing brewery and the family would live happily ever after. I couldn't tell her that I hated gardening, I was spending most of the money I earned on croissants and so far, I hadn't made a beer that was close to something someone would pay for.

It was time to make some tough decisions. I realised that my biggest outgoings were on croissants and booze. I was spending between twenty and thirty euros a week on croissants alone. I had lots of beer at home; the problem was a lot of it wasn't that drinkable/possibly a deadly nerve agent, but if I only drank the beer I made, that would save money, and also hopefully drive me to make better beer. I was spending quite a lot on wine, so I decided to cut out wine altogether. After thirty seconds of imagining life without wine I changed my mind and decided to only drink the cheap stuff. I got in touch with Fred, the local *vigneron*. He lives on a hill outside the village, on the way to Marigny-Marmande, and he looks a bit like Han Solo. He makes fizz that is absolutely shit hot for €4.50 a bottle, and he sells boxes of wine at €15 for ten litres. That would work out at just under €2 a bottle and it is better than any bottle you will get in the supermarket for under a tenner. I met Fred through the football team. I can't remember when, actually, so I presume it was after one of the veterans' matches when I was drunk. €15 ten litres of wine. It was perfect.

'It's still too bitter,' said Damien, tasting my latest attempt at my staple IPA.

'You make shit cars,' I muttered.

'What?'

'I said it's supposed to be somewhat bitter, Damien.' It tasted all right to me.

'It's too bitter for the French. All my friends say the same. You should try making a blonde beer.' We leant on his mini bar in his open-plan living room/kitchen, which was divided by a great stone arch that he had built (he had built a great stone arch!). Colleen was being told off by Celia for forging her signature on a school report card, which I thought was very impressive for a six-year-old. Unfortunately, she had spelt her mum's name incorrectly, otherwise she would have got away scot free and moved on to more sophisticated frauds.

'It's not bad though. It's better than the last time. I have a friend who wants to buy some,' continued Damien.

'Ah, well, I'm not signed up with my tax status yet, Damien, so I can't sell beer.'

'Yes, you can. Just don't tell anyone. He wants ten litres.'

'OK. Right. I'll sell them at three euros a litre.' I plucked a figure out of the air.

'No problem. I'll pick them up tonight when I drop off the fence posts,' he said. 'Have you thought about making a blonde?'

I didn't answer that. I was chuffed, though. I pretended the whole thing was a normal transaction and I was completely OK with it, but I was secretly delighted. Someone wanted to buy my beer! I was going to be rich! Thirty euros! That's about what it cost me to make ten litres of beer! Oh. Still, the beer was just about paying for itself, which was a start. What was particularly interesting was that Damien was still complaining that it was too bitter but people wanted to buy it. He liked it, I think. Indian pale ales or IPAs, the style of beer I was making, are bitter. They have loads of hops in them and that makes them bitter. Nowadays one uses techniques like whirlpooling and dry hopping (by now I had been reading books) to try get more flavour out of the hops without getting the bitterness, but IPAs will always be relatively bitter and that is a good thing as long as it's controlled. It gives a lovely crisp finish to the beer and balances it against the higher than usual alcoholic content and the maltiness. Normal French blonde beers use a very small amount of hops and are much smoother, a completely different style, so it is natural that if you tried an IPA like mine you would find it bitter. What I was hoping was that it was a question of the people round here getting used this new style. And the fact that they wanted to buy it suggested to me that this might be happening.

This was the first time I had sold beer, but I had already begun using it as currency. With the help of Damien I'd bought some fence posts from a local farmer because Rose wanted some sheep. Damien was delivering them for me in exchange for beer. I had also exchanged beer for the use of a battery charger, a pressure washer and, in one of my darker moments, I had tried desperately to exchange it for croissants at the local bakery when I ran out of cash.

I began to get a trickle of black-market beer customers. Pascal, the builder from down the road, was my best customer. One or two others, friends of Damien mostly. I started a smuggling route, hiding beers in the bottom of a pram my friend had given us for the impending birth of our child and pushing them over to Damien's house, where they would be distributed. I didn't make any money from it when I worked out how much it cost to make the beer, but it got my name out there.

As May rolled into June and the sun returned, we began to venture out again. Friends and relatives came to visit. We

61

would take them to Amboise, an old town on the Loire an hour to the east of us, where we'd get takeaway pizza and peruse the great market along the river, then head to the wine fair in the tunnels under the château to taste a thousand wines. Or we'd go to Blois, or Chenonceau or any of the incredible châteaux and towns on the Loire. As the evenings lightened, we would eat out on the veranda, me glugging Fred's red and Rose dreaming of a time after the baby was born when she too could glug Fred's red. The evenings made all the gardening worthwhile. Because there was little light pollution, the night sky was so much fuller than I remembered. Have you any idea how many stars there are? Somebody should do a count or something, because I am dying to know.

As far as I could tell, Rose didn't know why she wanted sheep. She didn't want to slaughter them, she didn't want to shear them and she certainly didn't want to milk them. She made it very clear she wanted sheep, though. I put it down to pregnancy cravings. Some people want to eat charcoal, some people want sheep. I wasn't entirely against the idea either; it would mean I wouldn't have to mow the orchard at the back of the house. What it did mean was I had to build a fence. This was my first big DIY project. It was the sort of task the farmers round here would send their children out to complete before going to school in the morning, but to me it was a test of manhood. A test of my virility. In preparation for the fence I had spent a lot of March and April in a life-or-death struggle with the swathes of brambles that covered the perimeter of the orchard.

I built the worst fence in Braslou. It took me two days and countless exotic swear words, but I built it out of wonky wooden poles and rolls of the cheapest wire fencing I could find, and I felt virile. It was so bad that farmers would stop in their tractors to marvel at it and take pictures, but still I felt virile. When the wind blew the fence rippled and swayed from one end of the garden to the other. But it was definitely a fence. A year before I wouldn't have been able to build a fence. I was starting to realise something important. Something that I could apply to my beer. And life I suppose, if you're going to be a hippy about it. If you just go out and try and do something and really persevere, the chances are you will get it done. It might be a shit version of whatever you are trying to do, but you can get it done. And the next time you will know what to do to make it better. Even if you've no idea where to begin, you've just got to get off your arse and start doing it and things will happen.

I'd never challenged myself before we moved over here. When you live in a big city and have a meaningless job it's hard to challenge yourself. It's easier to tick along. I bet millions and millions of people with beige jobs and beige lives don't ever challenge themselves, because when life ticks along like that you don't need to. But the thing is, to feel really, really virile, you do need to challenge yourself.

Virile. That is a creepy word.

The more I got to know Damien and Celia, the more interesting I realised they were. Damien was a stonemason, a man who worked with his hands. He was brutally honest. I think the French are more honest than the English in general because they worry less about hurting each other's feelings, but even for a Frenchman he was very straightfor-ward. But he also carved sculptures. He was an artist. While there is a significant amount of support for the far right in parts of rural France, Damien would rail against the racism and homophobia that existed in some provincial areas. He could be moody (I may be mistaking this for just being French), but then he would do anything for you, whether it meant putting himself out or not, and whether you asked him to or not. One day I found out he was learning the violin, for God's sake. Nobody plays the violin, do they? Well, do they?

Celia was an elegant, sophisticated woman who had previously lived in La Rochelle, a fashionable city on the west coast. She was a former showjumper but had somehow ended up in Braslou, like us. Braslou sucks you in. She was practical and hard-nosed and you got the feeling she would be the first to stick up for you in a fight. I don't know where they met, but here they were.

Everyone liked Damien and Celia. When you were at Damien and Celia's house there would be a constant stream of visitors calling in, friends, family, young and old, people from every part of society, having a beer and a cigarette and joking with Colleen. I have always been desperate to be liked, but I found the more you tried to be liked, the less people liked you. Damien didn't try. That's the secret, I think.

At the start of June, I visited Xavier's brewery, the Octopus Brewery on the edge of Orléans, situated in a large industrial building. I was immediately impressed with his set-up. He had professional signage outside and a well-stocked shop from which he sold all his beer. He stood behind a counter while a constant stream of customers came in and left with armfuls of booze. *I'd like to stand behind a counter. I bet I'd feel like ten thousand men*, I thought to myself.

Xavier gave me a tasting of his beers. They were

excellent. An award-winning brown Belgian Tripel and a crisp lager. I remarked on how big and professional his brewery was.

'You want to see the big professional brewery? Come this way . . .' he said.

We walked out of the back of the shop into a vast warehouse. I was expecting to see great towering vats bubbling with beer. I expected lots of people to be running around in white coats carrying hi-tech equipment, I had basically imagined it as some kind of laser-satellite laboratory owned and run by a Bond villain, but it was empty save for some bottles stacked in one corner and three metal pots on small stands, each about two feet in diameter, in the other corner.

'This is the big professional brewery!' he grinned, pointing at the pots.

'That's it?'

'That is it.'

I couldn't believe it. It was like finding out the Large Hadron Collider was powered by a monkey riding a bicycle.

'I could do this.' I said.

'It's such a simple system any idiot can make beer from it,' laughed Xavier.

'I could actually do this!' I said.

'The trick is making the beer taste good.'

'There's a very slim chance I could actually do this!' I said.

BEER NO. 5:
Sinister Turquoise Black IPA

Recipe

5.3 kg Maris Otter malt

250 g Chocolate malt

250 g Carafa special malt

100 g smoked wheat

10 g Nugget hops
at start of boil

1 kg Nugget hops 50
minutes into boil

Mistakes

Use of bittering hops
for flavouring

Overcooling wort

Not fermenting at
correct temperature

Becoming 75 per cent coffee

Creating a chemical
weapon so terrible it
is capable of altering
balance of world power

Naming children is trouble. It's enough to put you off the whole venture. We'd spent months barking names at each other over the coffee table and only succeeded in realising every name in the world was in some way fundamentally flawed. The problem was, how did you name someone when you didn't know what they looked like? So we resolved to wait until the birth. Then, we thought, once we saw our baby's face for the first time, a name would become obvious.

Finally, here we were in the delivery room in the aftermath of the most extraordinary event one could ever witness, staring at our newborn baby and deciding what to call him. Rose had powered through childbirth with the determination of an Essex smash-and-grab gang liberating a cash machine with the aid of a stolen bulldozer, while at the same time dealing with the whole experience with extraordinary dignity. I had cried like a lost child at a clown convention. It wasn't for me that I cried. It was when they handed her the baby. The joy in her expression, unfiltered by anything human. Actual pure joy. It kills me now thinking about it.

'Well, do you know his name?' I blubbed.

'Yes, I think so,' replied Rose. 'Do you?'

'Um. Wait. It's coming to me.' I stared at our baby intently. I examined every detail of his tiny, exquisitely formed face. What was his name? What really suited him? I closed my eyes and went into a deep trance. Rather than my nan's alarm clock, a fruit machine with names instead of symbols appeared in my head and began spinning furiously, until finally it stopped. And there, as I knew it would, a name manifested in my frontal lobe. A name that had been placed in my head by a greater power. It was so obvious now. It was the perfect name for him. I stopped blubbering and, staring at Rose, who had never looked more wonderful, I took a deep breath and placed her hand in mine, savouring the enormity of the announcement.

'Podgington Squeaker.'

'Podgington Squeaker?' said Rose.

'Yes Rose, he will be called Podgington Squeaker.'

'I was thinking more along the lines of Albert.'

'Oh, right. Albert. That's nice too. Let's call him

Albert.' I paused for a moment and shut my eyes. 'Squeaker McGookin.'

'What?'

'Nothing. Albert. Albert is a good name.'

The care in the hospital in Chinon was sensational. We had an en-suite room with a TV and a bed that you could raise up and down as you pleased. The food was excellent. They kept us in for five days – the norm over here for a first baby (we tried to stay longer, but they threatened to call the gendarmes). A constant stream of friendly midwives came in to coo over Albert. I'd heard terrible things about people giving birth in the hospitals in London: one midwife for ten patients, being left in a cupboard while they tried to find space, but in Chinon it was quite the opposite. It was like being at a spa. I expected to bump into Richard Branson walking down the corridor in a white flannel dressing gown with a face pack made of seahorse poo.

There were two sheep in our orchard when we arrived home from the hospital with Albert. I'd forgotten about them. On the morning Rose's waters broke, before we left for hospital, a farmer from down the road turned up with his daughter, a slight teenage girl who wrestled the sheep out of the van with a grip of iron and chucked them unceremoniously into our orchard while he tutted at the fence I'd constructed badly and the gate I'd constructed badly and my general appearance. Initially, I had thought the arrival of sheep must be some kind of sign that Rose was giving birth to the second coming of the Messiah, but then I remembered we had ordered them some time before as part of Rose's pregnancy cravings. We named them Barbara and Winifred. Barbara was confident and outgoing, but Winifred was bad tempered and would stamp her feet if you went too near her. I didn't hold it against her. I suspected it was due to deep-seated self-esteem issues.

Right, I thought, *this baby business is all well and good, but I'd better get back to brewing some beer. No time to waste. I'm going to be one of those modern parents who just carries on as normal, except with a baby strapped on their back.* But before I could, Albert began to cry.

Three months passed.

I'll tell you how we ended up buying the house. When we were planning our escape from London I was searching for places to rent on the internet. We had a place to stay for March in Brittany and a place for June to September in the Auvergne, but we needed somewhere for April and May. The place in March was owned by a friend of Rose's dad, so it was free, and the place in the Auvergne was pretty cheap. I found the advert for La Ruche, which was owned by a lady called Mishi, and it looked spectacular. It was more than we had planned to spend, but the other places were so cheap we thought we'd give it a go, and besides, we were flushed with redundancy money, and as everyone who's been made redundant knows, redundancy money never runs out.

I knew we'd like Mishi from the moment she changed my name. All I had enquired about was whether the house was available for rent and if she'd consider a reduction, as we were struggling writers/artists, and she'd sent several sprawling emails back covering topics from art history to recipe suggestions. And then she changed my name from Tom to Tommy, and she was right – I was a Tommy. It suited me. When I was young I was always a Tommy, it was only when I got older and life became difficult and boring that gradually I became a Tom to more and more people until only my closest friends called me Tommy. Mishi had a talent for putting things in the right place. She agreed to let us have the house for the months of April and May for a cut-price rate. 'Just do me a favour and mow the garden, sweetie,' she said. She hadn't mentioned the lawnmower was practically from a pre-combustion-engine era and the garden was actually a paddock.

The moment we walked through the rusted gates of La Ruche it was clear that one day we would buy it. Largely because Rose said, 'One day we will buy this house.' Mishi was in the kitchen waiting for us with a plate of ginger biscuits and the BBC World Service on the radio. She looked just like I'd imagined. There was something Narnia-esque about her. If someone had thawed out the White Witch and shown her the error of her ways, that would have been Mishi: regal, kindly, but every now and then with a flash in her eyes that said she wished she was still allowed to point at someone and turn them into ice. And you got the feeling that if she wanted to, she could. Not us, though. She seemed much taken with us.

'Tommy and Rosie! That could be the title of a children's programme. Come and have a biscuit.' She glanced at the bottle of wine that I was about to give her. 'Not for me, darling, I don't drink. Save it for yourself, sweetie. Honestly. Save it for yourselves.'

She had decorated the house beautifully. As I say, Mishi's great talent was that she just knew where things were meant to be. She walked us through the house, talking at a hundred miles an hour about every subject she could think of, pointing at walls and ceilings and doors and grand works of art on the wall that she had painted. She was a fantastic painter. The only rule was, there was to be no red wine in the bedrooms. But we could smoke dope up there if we wanted, she added, eying us carefully to see if we were the sort that smoked dope. The only thing she didn't comment on was a headless mannequin dressed in a nineteenth-century French gown on the landing. She breezed past it as if there wasn't a house in the world that didn't have one.

'You must come and meet us for coffee in the PMU in Richelieu. Maybe tomorrow morning? OK, bye, sweeties. Enjoy! Bye!'

Initially I wasn't as taken with La Ruche as Rose. I mean, the house itself was out of this world, but it was more the area. I'd pictured myself living atop a rocky cliff in Brittany or in an orange grove in Provence, but here the landscape was, at first glance, unspectacular. It was gentle. Quiet. Quiet except for one of the neighbour's dogs, which I think was a cross between a Rottweiler and an American wrestler. Also, to get anywhere you had to drive. I had imagined walking into the village to pick up my fourteen croissants for breakfast every morning. Finally, and most damning of all, as far as I could see, the house didn't have a wine cellar.

But over those two months the sun shone and the countryside gradually revealed its beauty, little hills and ridges that gathered and released like an unmade bed, and we discovered breathtaking châteaux and magnificent towns like Chinon and Saumur and, indeed, Richelieu. Through Mishi we met David and Ali Kimber Bates and they introduced us to everyone. I mean everyone. We would sit with Ali outside the PMU café and she would shout at people as they walked past and demand they come and meet us. Nobody dared refuse. And by the time we left it was a wrench, because it felt like we fitted the place.

Three months later we were staying in a Spartan cottage

in the Auvergne atop the gorge of the River Bouble, to this day my favourite river name (I like to imagine a baby Michael Bublé being washed up on its banks in a bed made of reeds and tuxedo, effortlessly crying the tune of 'Fly Me to the Moon' and thus melting the hearts of the local peasant women doing their washing, who at first wept and then threw giant peasant knickers). Our friend was visiting and we had gone for a day out at Volcania. Volcania is a volcano-themed fun park in the Auvergne. We'd been queuing for nearly an hour for the star attraction, a driverless bus tour round the car park, when Mishi rang.

'Tommy, darling, listen. The thing is, my estate agent has found a buyer for La Ruche, but at eighty thousand euros less than I wanted. Now, sweetie, I have to sell the place, we're down to our last pennies' – (she always says that!) – 'but if I have to sell at that price, I'd prefer to sell to you. I know how much you love the place and we really love you. Also, if I sell direct to you I won't have to pay the extraordinary estate agent fees.'

'Well, that's kind of you to think of us, but I'm afraid it's still rather out of our . . .'

'Tell her we'll buy it.' Rose interjected. She was listening in.

'What?' I said.

'Please, Tommy. Tell her we'll buy it. We'll be happy there. We'll find a way to afford it.' There was something in her voice, something her eyes, a wondrous look that said *if you don't get on board with this I will shove you into fast-moving traffic.*

'Mishi. We'll take it!'

'Marvellous sweeties both! I'll email you the details and what you need to do. Wonderful to have you back.'

And that was it. It was so easy. We went back to the Loire the next week to sign paperwork. We had a meeting with Mishi about what furniture from the house she was willing to sell. She argued with herself for an hour over tea and biscuits while we sat in silence, before drawing up a list and writing a price next to it, then arguing herself down on the price by about 20 per cent.

'Can we keep the four-poster bed?' I said when she was done. I'd always thought that if I had a four-poster bed Bonnie Tyler would like me, should I ever meet her. We'd become friends. Meatloaf too, probably. People like that.

'Of course you can, sweetie, because we can't get it out now without knocking down a wall. We built the loft conversion after we put the bed in. It doesn't fit through the door.'

That was all I needed to hear. Over the next few months Mishi emailed on a daily basis with changes to the list of furniture she was prepared to leave in the house, to the point where we had no idea whether there would be anything left when we moved in, but we knew we had the four-poster bed, and that was good enough for me, because in many ways I am a simpleton.

Rose sold her flat in London and added to that we used a sizeable chunk of our redundancy money. That gave us enough to buy the house outright. Even though it was more than we should have spent, the same house in London would have cost ten times what we paid. The only problem was it didn't leave us with much money to start our new life. Still, as long as there weren't any major life changes, we would be OK.

Nine months later, thanks in some part to the four-poster bed, Albert was born.

*

Generally speaking, hops do two things: on the one hand they release alpha and beta acids, which give the beer its bitter taste, and on the other hand they release various oils that give the beer its other flavours, which, depending on the hop variety, could be fruity flavours or herbal flavours, woody or mineral-like. There are hundreds of different oils in hops and we don't yet know what half of them do. But the point is some hops, like the Nugget variety, are very high in alpha acids and are therefore used primarily at the start of the boil to give the bitterness. It doesn't matter if they boil for a long time and the oils in them evaporate, as you aren't really looking to extract much flavour from them anyway, just the bitterness – the acids. Other hops, like the Citra variety, are lower in the acids but have much more flavour oils – in the case of Citra, citrus-like flavours. A remarkable coincidence. So you wouldn't normally put them in at the start of the boil, as at they aren't as effective at bittering as some hops, and all the oils that give the delicious flavours that Citra is known for will be evaporated by the time you get to the end of the boil. Instead, you put hops like this towards the end of the boil, or even after the boil, when the temperature is dropping, so that you don't lose too much of the oils.

I managed to do one final brew just before Albert was born. A smoked black IPA. In a moment of jubilance I threw in a kilogram of very bitter Nugget hops towards the end of the boil. I had this whole kilogram bag of Nugget hops and I just thought, *I'm going to chuck this lot in. It will probably be all right.* That was my thought process. This is the stage where you are supposed to use flavouring hops, not bittering hops. Also, normally I would use a hundred grams of a flavouring hop like Citra for twenty-five litres of beer. I used a kilo of Nugget hops. I managed to bottle it in a contrary state of caffeine-soaked exhaustion a couple of weeks after we had returned from the hospital, and two weeks after that it was ready to taste.

One of the best things about trying my beers out on Damien was that I learnt lots of new French vocabulary. On this occasion for instance, I had learnt that *révoltant* means revolting and *herbicide* means, well, you get the idea.

'It is much too bitter, but there is something else. Something even worse. Something terrible,' said Damien.

He was right. There was another flavour in there. Something not of this world. To this day I can't quite describe it in a way that means anything, other to say that it was a sinister, turquoise flavour. Sinister turquoise? What the hell does that mean? I know! But that's what it was. Sinister Turquoise. I had created something terrible. The sort of thing that, if the North Koreans got their hands on it, they could use to potentially destroy the world. Sinister Turquoise would be a good punk band name.

In total, I had made around eight or nine brews by now, many too uneventful to mention. But I was starting to realise that perhaps my beers weren't as good as I had initially thought. When you make your first beer, you're so overwhelmed by the success of making something that can genuinely get you pissed that you are blind to its faults. Gradually, as my beers progressed, I began to realise there were serious issues to be addressed. In the case of this smoked black IPA, it was simply a bad recipe. My fault. I was starting to experiment and I didn't really have a clue what I was doing, but at least I could fix it next time. But with my normal lighter IPA beers I had eventually been forced to accept that they all had an astringent taste that remained no matter how I altered the recipe. And yet my dark beers, even this disaster, didn't have it. Further reading was required. I knew that. The problem was, having a young baby meant I was so tired I could barely read the back of a shampoo bottle, let alone a chapter of a book.

I like to read the backs of shampoo bottles when I'm on the loo, you see. That's why I mentioned it. I find it relaxing. It's not a crime.

Our biggest error, as humans, is that we think we can control everything. We think that with science as our guide we can understand and master the world. What we fail to realise is that the world is fundamentally absurd, and no amount of knowledge can truly control it. Trying to tame nature is a fruitless exercise. This is what I used to believe until I met Monsieur Richard.

Monsieur Richard is the sort of man you can't help but respect. He holds himself in a way that commands respect. His first name is Christian, but you call him his formal name, Monsieur Richard, despite his protestations. He is in his late sixties, he has a voice that has dispensed with any unnecessary affectations and is low and sandy. He has great bear paws for hands, an immaculately trimmed beard, which he gets done once a week at the local hairdresser's, and he is a genuine, lovely man.

He doesn't have to be. I suspect he could be a complete arsehole and have everything he wants, because when you are in his presence it's like Godzilla is in the room. He could bully people to get what he wants. He could force his way to the front of every queue, but instead he is generous and kind. When anyone in the Richelais asks you where you live, you tell them you live opposite Monsieur Richard and instantly they know where you are. Everybody knows Monsieur Richard. He should have retired long ago, but he spends his time helping young people starting local businesses get off the ground.

He lives with his wife, Madame Richard, in a reasonably new house. It's a peculiarity of the French that despite all the fantastic old houses that lie empty, they aspire to live in modern houses on the edge of town. That is the dream. Consequently, you come across ancient villages full of character that are left to crumble, while on the outskirts several streets of brand new, benign, 'pavilion' style houses that range from reasonably pretty to ugly as shite are thriving. Apparently, this is partly to do with mortgage regulations. It's much harder to get a mortgage on old houses in France, especially if you are young.

The Richards' house is different, though. It is not built in among streets and streets of other new houses. It stands alone against the backdrop of the forest on land his family have lived on for at least six generations. It is homely and well designed. It's exactly how you should do it. This is typical Monsieur Richard. His favourite words are *propre* (proper, tidy or correct) and *impec* (shorthand for impeccable). These are the principles he lives by. He treats everything tangible in this manner – people, animals, wheelbarrows. There are no shortcuts.

By this point we knew the Richards to say hello to. We'd wave to each other over the road. Then, one day a month or two after Albert was born, they invited us over to their house for lunch.

When we arrived, Monsieur Richard gave us a tour of his garden. It was astonishing. Rows upon row of salads, courgettes, cornichons (which his wife, Marie, pickles and which make any cornichons you've had before taste like newspaper), peppers, spuds, tomatoes and every other vegetable alive were perfectly spaced, to the millimetre, along expertly turned soil with a professional watering system installed, which runs down each row. It was really something to behold. It was the Sistine Chapel of vegetable gardens.

'How do you keep the bugs off the vegetables? Do you use sprays?' said Rose.

'*Non*. If the garden is done properly, well laid out and well maintained, *tout est propre*, it takes care of itself,' said Monsieur Richard. It was then that I realised he had tamed nature.

The rest of his house was equally impressive. Perfectly cut lawns. Electric gates, doors and garage doors, all controlled by one remote controller. Inside was spotless. All the furniture belonged exactly in its allocated space. There was a coffee table that unfurled into a drinks cabinet as if it was designed by the man who makes James Bond's equipment. Everything was quality. Nothing had been done on the cheap. *Propre. Impec.*

Marie had cooked a very traditional lunch. First, *apéros*. A sweet wine called Coteaux du Layon, which I absolutely love. It's a Loire wine from the Anjou region further west of us. Then we started with a red cabbage and duck gizzard salad. Gizzards sound horrible, but the way Marie cooked them they were delicious. I think it's just the name – gizzard. No one wants to eat something called a gizzard. They should call them something more appealing, like stomach truffles. That needs work, but it's undeniably a start. You simply can't deny that. Then we had juicy slices of beef with green beans cooked with garlic. In England now it's

78

all about cooking vegetables for the minimum time possible, so that they still have their crunch. Big mistake in my book, because the less you cook a vegetable, the more it tastes like a vegetable. Marie cooks her beans properly so that they are soft and have taken on all the flavour of the garlic. I could have eaten mountains of them. Then we had a cheese course – local Sainte-Maure de Touraine AOC goats' cheese, which is famed throughout France, blue cheese from the Auvergne and a Camembert. And for pudding a frangipane. Everything was exactly as it should be. *Impec.* It was all delicious.

The best bit about the Richards, though, and this is why I will always love them, is that although they had effectively tamed nature, they had mastered the art of living, they had completed the computer game of life, when they came to our house the next day and saw Burt digging holes in the lawn, bits of fencing and old dog beds strewn across the garden and the general chaos that envelops a house when you have a baby, they didn't judge us. They may have pitied us a little but they didn't judge us. Like Damien and Celia, they wanted to help us.

For the first few months after having a baby, coffee is your life drug. It replaces sleep. It replaces food, water. You live in a space between the conscious and the unconscious – a blur of midnight feeds and anxious conversations about vividly coloured poo. Vivid Poo would be a good name for a band. Your living room becomes a minefield of shrill musical toys that explode into double-speed nursery rhymes when you accidentally tread on them as you stagger around in your pants at 3 a.m. endlessly rocking the baby. You devote all your senses to monitoring the baby at all times. Everything else is impossible. When the baby doesn't sleep, you don't sleep. When the baby does sleep, you don't sleep because every thirty seconds you can't help but check they are breathing. The only way to cope is to make sure your body is made up of at least 50 per cent espresso. You've got to be careful not to overdo it, though – it can have side effects.

'The atmosphere in Richelieu was tense, Rose,' I said on returning from the bakery one day in August, having bought two croissants for us and two secret croissants just for me to eat in the car on the way home.

'Why?' said Rose, absent-mindedly holding a dribbling Albert.

'There's a new 1999 Renault Mégane estate in town.'

'What?'

'Previously there were just two of us, both white 1999 Renault Mégane estates. He stayed on his side of town and I stayed on mine. It wasn't ideal, but we coped. But now, a green 1999 Renault Mégane estate has turned up. Green, of all things! Parked outside my bakery in broad daylight. I eyeballed the driver as I rolled past it as if to say, "Let's meet at noon and try and shoot each other." The woman behind the wheel seemed a little frightened.'

'Yes . . . I'm not sure that's really a big deal?'

'OK, Rose, fine. Not a big deal. Nothing to worry about. Well, all I can say is don't come running to me when Richelieu is chock-full of 1999 Renault Mégane estates. 1999 Renault Mégane estates as far as the eye can see, taking our parking spots. Wall-to-wall 1999 Renault Mégane estates causing traffic jams, blocking fire hydrants. Bloody Renault Mégane estates running over elderly ladies and stealing our women, Rose. Those shitting 1999 estates, eating our croissants, Rose. EATING OUR

CROISSANTS, ROSE! EATING OUR FUCKING CROISSANTS, FOR CHRIST'S SAKE, ROSE. Eating our fucking croissants. Don't come running to me because I am telling you now – it's fucking happening. THEY ARE COMING, ROSE. They are coming.'

'Maybe you should cut down on the caffeine.'

'Yeah, you're probably right.'

After a crappy first half of the year, it got really hot from July to September. Mid- to high thirties most days. A proper heatwave like the ones you remember from your childhood – dry, endless, so hot you couldn't leave the house in the middle of the day or you'd be baked onto the landscape like a burnt cookie. Our once vibrant lawn was reduced to desperate little islands of brown grass surrounded by large patches of barren sandy soil. There are only a few things I remember from that time. Firstly, a goat arrived. I don't know why we got a goat. Rose wanted him for some reason. I presumed it was part of Rose's pregnancy cravings, which was odd because she'd already given birth. The goat was called Bevington. Sadly, and this is a very serious issue that I think it's important to discuss, Bevington turned out to be a misogynist, so after a week or so we had to get rid of him. He bullied Barbara and Winifred and he headbutted Rose's sister. My point is, there's no place for domestic violence in the modern world, even if you're a goat.

The only other event I really remember from that period with any clarity was finally going to my compulsory *stage de gestion* four-day management course in August. This was the course I had been booked on in April that I needed to complete in order to get my tax status as a brewer and gardener. Anyway, I thought it was a four-day management course, but it turned out I was booked onto a four-day argument.

On the first day, I walked into the meeting room in the Chambre de Métiers office in Tours, where the course took place, to find everyone sitting in horseshoe formation, screaming furiously at each other. In the centre a formidable little woman called Julia, who seemed to be in charge, took on all comers from around the horseshoe like a travelling-circus prize fighter, and there we remained all morning, shouting at each other. On Monday afternoon we all went into a conference room where another man stood in front of us and argued even more furiously with my classmates. We spent Tuesday morning back in the horseshoe, this time with Julia more confident than ever. She'd got the measure of us the day before. We started the day arguing about the previous afternoon's conference-room argument. This continued until Wednesday, when the arguing finally stopped. It stopped because Julia dedicated the entire day to explaining what would happen to your business if you got divorced. Suddenly my classmates were all ears. They sat in silence, anxiously taking notes. In a 2014 survey, 57 per cent of French men admitted to having affairs. Once she had finished this particular segment, the arguing began again.

The course was a perfect example of French bureaucracy. Julia spoke much too quickly for me to understand. I don't blame her: it wouldn't have been fair on all the other people in the class if she spoke at half speed. But the course was compulsory, regardless of whether I understood it or not. There was no exam, so I didn't have to understand it, but I did have to sit in a room full of arguments for four days without really knowing what was going on, just to get my certificate. And it wasn't only me. I got the impression that a lot of the French people on the course thought it was a waste of time. Here was a room full of young, motivated people (and me), desperate to get out there and start their new businesses, but before they could, they had to sit through four days of compulsory bullshit. This goes on all over the country every month. When you think about all that time wasted when people could be out there running their businesses and paying taxes, the French state must lose millions in potential revenue.

On a similar course in the UK everyone would sit in silence, meekly scribbling notes on their pads, never to be used again. Then, when they were a safe distance away, they'd complain bitterly to each other about what a waste of time it was. In fact, this is exactly what I am doing now. Not the French, though. They love to argue. They long to feel the garlic-tinged spittle of a furiously shrugging adversary flecking against their cheeks. They scream at each other, but then a few moments later they are all friends again.

It's probably a good thing. They don't bottle things up like the English do, and by arguing you hopefully arrive at some kind of truth. The only thing is, I assume in France – as in the UK – there is a substantial number of people who are morons. In the UK, although a lot of people who might have something interesting to say end up keeping their mouths shut, thanks to our nation's loving embrace of repression, it also means a high proportion of morons keep their mouths shut for the same reason. In France it's the opposite. Everyone is discussing things all the time. Clever people and morons. I'm not sure which is best. You might think it's better to have the morons blathering on if it means sensible people are voicing their opinion as well, but then there's nothing more frustrating than an argument between morons, is there? It's like watching people trying to play tennis with rolling pins.

I noticed something funny on my course. My classmates would sometimes say English phrases in what they thought was an English accent. 'Bye bye!' or, 'Let's go!' Things like that. They couldn't quite master an English accent, though, so they ended up sounding like a cartoon character. Bugs Bunny, normally. I found this hilarious until I realised that it was probably the same the other way round, so when I speak in what I think is a French accent it must sound equally ridiculous, and whereas they are just saying the odd English phrase, I am talking in French the *whole time*. For Damien and Celia, an evening with Rose and me speaking French must be like being stuck in a Warner Brothers cartoon omnibus.

From July to September I gardened as much as I could, baby permitting, getting out early, wacked up on coffee, and coming home a few hours later before the temperature reached 40°C, perforated by horseflies and mosquitoes, to find Rose and Albert in a darkened room with all the shutters shut and between eight and ten fans strategically placed around the sofas, rumbling away. There we would sit each afternoon, not daring to go out until sundown.

The days were hard, but the evenings were joyous. Still hot from the midday inferno, we spent early evenings in hammocks, rocking the baby under the shade of the trees in the dell, drinking Fred's fizz with cassis and eating mustard-flavoured crisps and then, as the sun set, we'd move onto the terrace and barbecue the absolute vitamins out of anything that seemed edible while *Exile on Main St* by the Rolling Stones played on repeat. If the baby slept, we'd play thousands of games of rummy on the wooden table outside the kitchen till late, surrounded by candles jammed into old wine bottles as bats swooped above us. At night Albert slept in the bed with us, all the windows open, trying to coax in any sort of a breeze. When I say he slept, I mean he slept in one- or two-hour stints, his waking up expertly timed to coincide with the exact moment when we were just falling asleep. It was a confusing, magical, exhausting time.

We began to emerge from the chaos of having a newborn baby around the start of October. It was amazing that when I looked back at the gardening over the summer, I realised I had actually done rather well. I hadn't really made any money on my black-market beers, but despite my ineptitude at gardening, I had gathered more and more clients, largely, I believe, out of sympathy and/or the twisted fascination that comes with watching a simpleton struggle with the most facile tasks – watching me work was like watching prehistoric man banging rocks together to see what would happen. But I found myself turning a profit. I had managed to save up around €1,000. I had also managed to get my tax status approved, I had registered with the Douane, the French Revenue & Customs, and I had been granted a licence to sell beer at the markets. All I needed now was the beer. There is a lot you need when you have a child, and I'm not just talking about hard liquour: there's all the cots and clothes and general apparatus that you have to have with a baby, which could add up to be expensive – but both Rose's sisters and my brother had children, so in fact we had a surplus of baby things. We had everything at least twice over – cots, car seats, a million items of clothing.

I brewed once or twice after Albert was born, and the results weren't spectacular. I have already mentioned the herbicide black IPA, but my normal IPA beers, the ones I was hoping would be my main selling beer, were still coming out with an astringency that wasn't particularly pleasant.

Nevertheless, after a summer of gardening, once I had put a croissant quota into place and substituted Fred's red for expensive supermarket wines, I now had some cash in my pocket. I started to look around for breweries. You can pick up a pico brewery (a very small microbrewery) for around €1000. That would make 100 litres of beer a time. This wasn't enough for a commercial venture really, but it was all I could afford. I told myself if I brewed twice a day, every day, I might be able to make some money. Twice I found breweries for sale on the internet, but both times when I phoned up to enquire, they had already been sold. I began trawling the internet obsessively.

At the end of September Celia gave birth to Zoe, an beautiful baby with eyes that gleamed and twinkled. For Braslou, alongside Albert this amounted to a population explosion.

We travelled back to England in late October for my mum's seventieth birthday. She hired a house in Southwold on the east coast of England. My mum is the eldest of thirteen brothers and sisters, all of them lovely people and all of them, to a person, quite, quite mad. My uncle Mark eats five kilograms of cheese a week. Aunty Maggs is an ex-lawyer, ex-property developer, ex-around-the-world sailor who used to live on a boat and now lives on a house on the edge of a cliff that is eroding daily. Aunty Myra makes a living buying things at car boot sales and selling them on eBay, and she drinks nothing but coffee and red wine. Mostly red wine. I think she drinks coffee to rehydrate. There are loads of others, all insane. I bored them all with my plans to by a brewery.

I hinted that I might need some investment, but none of them seemed interested.

When we got back to France at the end of October, we were caught out. The seasons had changed. It was cold. Seasons feel more defined here. They change overnight. Suddenly summer was over. As the evenings got colder we started having log fires, but they weren't enough to keep the house warm. I remembered how cold it got the winter before – Rose and I huddling as close to the fire as we could without losing our eyebrows. We wrapped Albert up in more and more layers. It wasn't right. It was only going to get colder and I knew we had to do something. I was continuing to search for microbreweries, but I was starting to realise that the money I had saved might be about to be repurposed. I received an email on 16 November, the day before my birthday:

> Tommy, I am upgrading to a larger a brewery and I therefore have a 100-litre brewery for sale. €1000 to you. To be honest, it's a pain in the arse brewing with something that small, I would suggest getting something bigger, but if you want it, it's yours.
> Cordialement
> Xavier

If I'd received the email a month before, I would have bought it, but now the pressure was on. Rose had been dropping hints like:

'We should get a log burner.'

And:

'Why haven't we got a log burner yet?'

And:

'Your son is freezing to death. We need to spend the money on a log burner.'

Some I picked up on, some were probably too subtle, but I knew things were about to come to a head.

We visited Beauval ZooParc for my birthday, about an hour east of Braslou. It was raining. I always think I want to go to zoos, but when I get there I find them depressing. The animals look bored and I find it hard not to take this personally. Beauval was a sort of unreconstructed zoo. No great expanses for the lions and tigers to roam in; instead they repeatedly patrolled small patches of grass surrounded by flimsy-looking fencing so that their footprints were worn into the dirt, just desperate for something to happen, surrounded by an endless line of wide-eyed, slack-jawed morons with nothing better to do with their lives than sneer at some poor creature less fortunate than themselves. It reminded me of my teenage years in north Hertfordshire.

Albert, now four months old, wasn't the least bit interested in the suicidal big cats. He saw every outing as an opportunity to sleep. He was sleeping when we rolled him (in a pram) into the one canteen that was open on a wet November Thursday in Beauval ZooParc.

'Look, Tommy, we've got to do something about the house. I know you've been saving the money for the brewery, but we're not going to get Albert through the winter if we don't get some sort of heating.'

'You know what creates a lot of heat, Rose?'

'A log burner?'

'Well, yes. But also, and this is interesting, did you know that microbreweries often have two or even three heated tanks? Now, there must be some relatively straightforward way to harness . . .'

'We're getting a fucking log burner,' said Rose.

'Good idea.'

Reluctantly I replied to Xavier that I wasn't in a position to buy his little brewery system. Although this was almost certainly the end of my scheme to start a brewery, at least for this year, when I gave it some thought it felt like a relief. I didn't know anything about running a brewery. I liked telling people that I was going to start a brewery; it was something to say and so often I had nothing to say, but I'm not sure I ever thought I would really start one. Despite this, it was the only plan I had left, and now it was gone I felt empty. I'd given up on the murder-mystery book. I'd sent it to every agent in the UK without success, so I had changed the title of the book and sent it to all the agents again, hoping they wouldn't remember, but that hadn't seemed to work either. It was almost as if I had written a really, really bad murder-mystery book.

It was a comedy/murder mystery that I assumed would be the next *Harry Potter*, but even though I sent it out to all the publishers I could find, I received zero responses. Finally, after badgering a particular publisher with emails and eventually calling them, I had this conversation.

'But you publish lots of murder mysteries – what's wrong with mine?' I said.

'Well, the problem with it really is that it's quite obvious who committed the murder within the first three pages. So it's not much of a mystery.'

'Oh. It's a comedy as well, though. You publish lots of comedies.'

'Yes. No. The other problem is it's not really very funny, which makes it not much of a comedy.'

'Oh. Well, what is it, then?'

Long pause.

'It's words. It's just lots of words.'

As much as I hated it, I could start gardening again in the new year, and with Rose bringing in some money from selling sculptures and her marketing job, we could get by for a bit, but I couldn't garden for ever. We would limp on, but it was starting to feel like our life in France wasn't going to be sustainable.

Great January downpours dragged through Richelieu Forest by a bitter wind left the landscape translucent and anaemic, before finally arriving onto my sad little head. It wasn't only the weather that was *desperate* in Braslou.

I brewed a lot over winter. There was little else to do. With the glorious summer over, we were forced indoors. I focused on IPAs, but I also made porters, stouts and Belgian ales. Think of this as the *Rocky* training montage bit. I experimented with different malts and hops and I discovered that, instead of having to buy most of my hops from America, I could buy Cascade and Nugget hops, both excellent for IPAs, grown in the Alsace region of France. Not only that, I also discovered new and interesting varieties of German hops that worked well in IPAs and other beers. This all made sense. I wanted to make a beer that was modern – and by that I mean a craft beer IPA, not an easy-drinking blonde lager – but there didn't seem much point in copying an American-style IPA completely, because that would mean I would be entering into direct competition with all the other millions of IPAs out there, and there are so many exceptional IPAs.

So I wanted a European take on it, using European hops. The more French, the better, but German hops would do as well. The problem was, no matter what hops I used, I was still getting a strange aftertaste with the IPA. I started brewing Belgian Abbaye beers too. Abbaye beers are strong beers, like Leffe, traditionally brewed by Belgian monks with a particular yeast that gives them a flavour of cloves and bananas. I'd spent several happy mornings down at Bruno's bar in Braslou with Damien drinking Leffe, so I thought I'd start by creating something like that. They also came out reasonably well, those Belgian beers, but they had the same aftertaste. Indeed, the only beers I made that didn't have the astringent aftertaste were the dark beers. The porters and stouts.

I forced myself to read some of the denser chapters of *How to Brew*, I listened to hours and hours of beer-related podcasts, and eventually I decided the problem was the water. More specifically, the pH level of the water. Ideally, in the mash, you want the pH level to be between 5.2 and 5.5. You see, different styles of beer are suited to different water types. For instance, the pilsner style of beer (from a town called Pilsen in the Czech Republic) developed in an area where the water is extremely soft, so they could use very light-coloured malts, which don't affect the pH balance and produce a balanced beer. Stouts, on the other hand, with their darker, roasted malts, which lower the pH level in the wort, developed in areas with water that contained a lot of bicarbonates, so that the dark malts balanced out the bicarbonates in the water. This was the case in Braslou. The water was very high in bicarbonates. That could have been what was giving my beer these 'off' flavours. I needed to add darker malts to balance out the bicarbonates.

Now, the chemists among you may have spotted in this last paragraph that I don't really have a clue what I am talking about, and that much of what I said is scientifically incorrect. But it's not entirely my fault. Understanding the chemical composition of water is like trying to solve a crossword with the clues written by Mr Blobby. How can adding calcium sulphide to water reduce the alkalinity when calcium is alkaline? Is there calcium in calcium sulphide? If you know the answer to that, then just fuck off. And some of what I said is true, by the way, for those of you sniggering at the back. It is to do with bicarbonates. And stouts and pilsners and the like did develop because of the different levels of minerals in the waters. But that's all I can fathom. What was clear was this: darker malts worked better where I lived. Therefore, I needed to make beers using darker malts.

I didn't want to only make stout, though. I like IPAs like Big Job. I wanted to make IPAs. And I like Abbaye beers like Leffe. You can artificially alter the chemical composition of the water to suit different beers using various menacing-looking white powders – indeed, most breweries do this if they are not lucky enough to be sitting on the right type of water in the first place – but this seemed like cheating to me. I wanted my beer to be sucked from the very earth I stood on. The answer, I decided without any research whatsoever, was to make a red IPA. Greenwich Meantime Brewery make a beer called Yakima red and it is one of my favourites. I was pretty sure that they were getting the red colour in their beer by using darker malts, maybe Munich malt, which is darker than a standard pale-ale malt, but not properly roasted like a chocolate or Carafa malt, which you might use to make stout. Hopefully, if I used the right amount of Munich malt it would be dark enough to counterbalance the bicarbonate in the water (stop sniggering at the back). I presumed this would work with Abbaye beers as well. You get darker Abbaye beers too. Leffe make a brown beer. There were loads of them. And so I started adding more dark malts.

Initial results were positive. The acrid aftertaste disappeared in both the IPA and the Belgian Abbaye. All of a sudden I was starting to make beers that were good. As well as this, I experimented with dry hopping my stout with Mandarina Bavaria hops to give them an aroma of orange. I should explain dry hopping. Normally you add your hops on the day you brew the beer when the wort (the liquid that will become beer) is boiling, but when you dry hop you add the hops several days after the brew day, when the beer is fermenting in the fermenter or even when it has fermented and is in the keg. By adding the hops at this late stage, and letting them sit in the beer for a few days, you get a really strong hoppy flavour, but without getting the bitterness. It's how they make the powerfully hopped American IPAs. It doesn't necessarily have to be an IPA, though. You can dry hop anything. People often think it's a new technique invented recently by trendy American microbreweries, but it's not. It's a technique that started in England a while back. I'm going to say 1892 but, between you and me, I have no fucking idea. Old English brewers would put a little plug of hops in the cask just before they sealed it so that when it was opened it would give a blast of fresh hops. That's how dry hopping started.

The beers weren't perfect – the IPA was under-hopped, the Belgian beer had too much Munich malt and the stout was too bitter – but these were fixable by simple adjustments. They were interesting beers. Drinkable beers.

Michael, an English builder we'd met at a dinner party at Mishi's house, fitted the wood burner for us. Michael is the sort of person who is a godsend when you move to France. Firstly, he is a lovely man who would go out of his way to help you. Secondly, he's been here for fifteen years or more, he speaks excellent French, he knows all the tradesmen, he knows how much everything should cost and therefore he can tell you immediately if someone is trying to rip you off.

The wood burner transformed the house. There's lots of advice about how to calculate the size of wood burner you need to heat your living room, but it involved equations and, well, you've read enough by now to know that wasn't going to work out, so I just bought the biggest one we could afford. I probably should have done the equations because it proved to be as hot the centre of the sun. At full power it was so strong that although it was situated in the living room, we'd be forced to stand against the far wall of the kitchen next door, as far away as was physically possible while remaining in the house to stop ourselves being incinerated. There were times in January when we would have all the windows on the ground floor open just to try and stop from overheating.

Naming beer is difficult nowadays. The problem is, people always take things too far. I don't like the direction the craft beer movement is going in. There's an element in craft brewing who are obsessed with the numbers behind beer. They want to turn it into an exact science. They want to calculate everything to death. If you listen to them talk, in minutes you'd be convinced they'd worked out the equation for the perfect pint. That they could punch all their numbers into a computer and some kind of godly IPA would pour out of the USB port. Message boards on craft beer forums are full of these twats trying to out-number-crunch each other. There are beer labels now that have so much information on them – the number of IBUs (International Bitterness Units), clarity level, the SRM (Standard Reference Method) colour value – that they look more like the results of an MRI scan. There are organisa-tions that produce definitions of what a beer style should be. Each style should be of a certain bitterness, a certain malt balance, a certain colour, otherwise they are not correct. Well, fuck you, dorks. This happens with everything. It's something certain types of men do to make themselves feel better about their miniature cocks. They overanalyse, they like to think they are in control of it all. They want everyone to know they have the answers and they are the bestest. I mean, just shit off. I am not interested. I hate this approach for three reasons:

We are talking about taste. It's subjective. You can't create the perfect beer because no one would agree on it.

It takes all the fun out of it. Numbers take the fun out of everything. Have you ever done a jigsaw with an account-ant? Me neither. Sounds dull as fuck though, doesn't it? Beer making should be about smelling, tasting, experimenting. Not sitting on a carousel, shitting numbers all over a giant Excel spreadsheet.

If you follow this philosophy it means you are signing up to a world of preciseness. A digital world of 1s and 0s. You are devolving responsibility for the flavour of your beer to a calculator, and last time I checked, calculators don't drink beer (I haven't checked, but I'm fairly certain this is still true*).

It was this sort of thinking that led to giant industrial breweries ruining beer for the best part of a century. I want to brew in the moment. I want my beers to taste different each time. I want beers to reflect the mood I was in when I made them. God, even writing this is making me feel alive. Death to technology! Not Nespresso machines, though. They have definitely added value to the world. But death to everything else!

I decided that I would have no part in these current trends. If I ever came to start selling beer properly, I would call my principal beer Braslou Bière and nothing more. Perhaps it was an IPA, but I didn't want to get into classifying my beers because it wasn't a straight IPA. I decided not to list anything more than I was legally obliged to on the label. I couldn't have given less of a fuck what IBU rating it had. Whether its SRM colour level was not sufficient for an IPA was as important to me as the colour of John Major's undercrackers.

---

* Calculators don't have mouths, that's my reasoning.

BEER NO. 6:

Electrocuted Chicken Porter

RECIPE	MISTAKES
4.5 kg Pale malt	Not enough mouthfeel
400 g Chocolate malt	Allowing too much oxygen into the beer when bottling
300 g Roasted barley	
20 g Nugget hops at start of boil	Not electrocuting Burt enough
50 g Mandarina Bavaria hops in fermenter	General insanitariness
	Trying to fit a quarter of a ton of malt into a toy car
	Pushing Louis to commit a terrible act

I suppose we started electrocuting our animals around Christmas time. We began with the dogs, of course. The problem was we were going to England for three weeks over Christmas and New Year and we were planning to leave the dogs in France (with a house-sitter, before you phone the RSPCA, who wouldn't be able to help anyway because they are not French – *touché*) and they'd started jumping over the fences, so we had to try and keep them in.

How Burt managed to jump the fences was bewildering – he was as fat as can be, but he was managing it and we had to do something. So we bought this wire that you bury underground and collars that gave them a shock if they got too close to the wire. It scared the shit out of them. It was awful. It is wrong to electrocute animals, I know that, but we had to do it or the dogs would have escaped onto the road and been hit by a car. But it didn't end there because, as anyone who has done this will know, electrocuting your animals is addictive. By the time February came round we were in full swing, electrocuting everything we could lay our hands on.

In March a miniature horse arrived, something to do with Rose's pregnancy cravings, which was odd, because Albert was now nine months old, so it seemed only right that we bought another electric fence so we could electrocute him too. Joyously, we realised if we put the sheep in with the horse then we could electrocute them as well. It was only the chickens that we didn't electrocute. And not for the want of trying, let me tell you. When I think back to it, I wonder if I could have wired them up to a faulty toaster.

The horse was delivered by an extraordinary woman called Valérie – a character straight out of some kind of American soap opera. She wore fur coats and drove around in a bright pink horse carrier, and she had a way of charming you while treating you with complete disdain. She charged us an outrageous price for the miniature horse, but it was very hard to say no to her. Even when she insisted on taking one of our sheep as petrol money.

The horse was a Falabella called Gadget. Falabellas are a miniature breed. The thing was tiny, the size of a fat Alsatian dog. But, as Rose explained to me, he was still a

98

stallion because he was an uncastrated male. In fact, once you got to know him, you realised he was a proud stallion. He held his head high, he trotted with the pomposity of an emperor and he galloped around the field as if, in his head, he was some kind of thoroughbred racehorse. I liked him and began to mimic his body language when I was around the town. He didn't like me much though, because every time I went near him, he tried to bite me.

'Try breathing up his nose. That will calm him down,' suggested Rose as he stomped his hooves at me one day while I tried to pat him on the head.

'OK, I'm doing it. Does he look calmer?'

'Well, he's certainly warming to you.'

'How can you tell?'

'He seems to be getting aroused. You're arousing him.'

'I'm arousing him? Is that good?'

Before Rose could answer, I found out it wasn't good. Gadget reared up at me (this sounds more frightening that it actually was: he only came to about my waist) and tried to mount me. I ran, of course, and Gadget chased me round the field for several minutes, determined to hump me.

And that, my friends, was the time I was sexually molested by a miniature horse.

At the end of February, I took samples of my new beers over to Damien and Celia's for tasting. Damien happened to be holding an exhibition of his sculptures at his house. The whole of the open-plan ground floor was full of magnificent stone carvings of all shapes and sizes.

Colleen was in trouble because Damien had left her in his truck while he nipped into the supermarket and when he came out an angry mob had formed. It transpired that every time someone walked past the truck, Colleen had given them a polite wave and a loud blast of the horn, which, being on a truck, was basically a slightly scaled-down version of a foghorn. Several people had apparently screamed and dropped their shopping. Colleen's defence was that she was just being friendly.

There were several people there, including the Mayor of Braslou, Madame Leclerc. I was desperate for them to taste my beers because I thought they were pretty good.

We started off with the Braslou IPA.

'It's too bitter, but it's nice,' said Damien.

'Shit cars.'

'What?'

'I said "thanks".'

'It's brilliant,' said Rose. 'It smells of oranges and pine.'

We moved onto the Belgian beer.

'But it's fantastic!' said Celia.

'It's really good,' said Damien. 'You could sell this, you know.'

'If I had a proper brewery I would.'

'But why can't you sell the beer you're making now at the market?' asked Celia.

'Because I'm not making anywhere near enough. My equipment is home-brew equipment. It's not for commercial use.'

'But you have all your authorisations. You're tax-registered; you're registered with revenue and customs. How much can you make in one go? Forty bottles?'

'Well, after racking it off, I'm normally left with twenty to twenty-one litres. At thirty-three centilitres per bottle, that's around sixty bottles.'

'And how many times a month can you brew?'

'I have three fermenters and the beer sits in them for two weeks, so six times a month if I really had the time.'

'So you could make three hundred and sixty bottles a month!' said Damien.

'You know it's the *marché de l'asperge* in April? If you can make enough beer, you can have a stall there if you want,' interjected Madame Leclerc.

'Well, yes, I suppose I could, if I had the time,' I said.

Damien stifled a scoff. He has a very different work ethic from me. Damien heads off to work at 7.30 a.m., gets home at 6 p.m., and then tends to his vegetables, his animals, his various building projects, his sculptures and his children. This is a man who has never wasted a minute of his life. I knew it would be futile arguing the importance of spending forty-five minutes of quality time alone every evening, centring myself, both spiritually and physically, on the loo. So I ignored him and continued, 'I mean I could do the market, yes. If you think the beers are good enough. I doubt I would make any money because I'm producing on such a small scale.'

'You could sell them at two euros a bottle,' said Celia.

'Because they are so good?'

'No. You just say they're artisan beers. if you say anything is artisan, that means you can overcharge for it.'

'Oh, right. Thanks. I'd have to get labels for the beers and more bottles and stuff. But it might be worth it.'

'I'll help you,' said Damien. 'I know everyone in the village. I'll get loads of people to buy your beer. You'll have no problem selling it.'

'Really? It's going to be a morning's work, at least.'

'Yes. No problem. I'll man the stall with you. We can use my truck. We'll load it up with your beer the night before and drive it down in the morning. I even have a mini bar that we can use to serve from.'

'Well, that's brilliant. Let's do it!'

'OK, but we'll need aprons with "Braslou Bière" printed on them.'

'We'll need aprons?'

'Yes. I'm not doing it without an apron with "Braslou Bière" on it.'

'OK, Damien. No, absolutely. We'll get aprons.' To this day I don't know why Damien insisted on getting branded aprons, but I was into it. I once read that for a period during the early 1980s Blackie Lawless, lead singer of the rock band W.A.S.P., would utilise an exploding codpiece to give his stage act that certain *je ne sais quoi*. Ever since then I had always wanted my own exploding codpiece, but the inherent danger of hanging dynamite around one's nuts had put me off. No, a branded apron, while still equally as rock and roll as an exploding codpiece, seemed more, I don't know ... more *me*.

There isn't a better-groomed man on the planet than Claude Capaval. Capaval isn't his real surname, it's the name of his business, I think, but it suits him. It gives him the air of a chivalrous knight. I met him on the terrace of the bar in Cravant. Cravant is the best winemaking village in the Chinon denomination. It's a linear village, like so many of the villages in the area, strung out for kilometres along one road just above the flood plain of the Vienne, surrounded by vineyards. Interestingly, on the opposite side of the river is the village of Tavant. It's nice that they made it rhyme. I once had a pen pal from the village of Tunting in the east of France. Sadly, they didn't ever adopt the same naming policy for the village opposite Tunting. Actually, that would have made it Crunting. That's less funny than I had hoped.

I knew Claude would be an interesting guy. When I phoned him to arrange the meeting, he hadn't picked up, but his answerphone message sounded like an acceptance speech for a Nobel Prize and he had a voice of 10,000 sexual conquests, so I thought I might like him. So when a man in his forties with long grey hair, perfectly coiffed like David Ginola, designer glasses with bright blue rims, smart jeans and a gilet over an immaculately pressed striped shirt, all completed by an enormous pink cravat, strode out of the bar sipping from an espresso cup and holding the saucer up to his chin, I knew he was my man. I also instinctively knew I would buy my labels from this man, regardless of whether he was the cheapest supplier or not. And it turned out he was not the cheapest. In preparation for the market I'd met several other label printers: all were perfectly nice, at least one was cheaper than Claude, but, when I explained to them that I probably wasn't very interesting to them as I only needed a small number of labels, they didn't stare into my soul and say in a voice that was so sexy it could probably reverse a vasectomy: 'It doesn't matter to me how many labels you want. I exist to meet people, to help people. I exist to help you.'

I already knew what I wanted to my labels to look like. I'd had an image in my head for many months. They would be very simple. Gold lettering printed directly onto the bottle, or onto a transparent label, so it looked like the lettering was printed directly onto the bottle. And it would say 'Braslou Bière'. And that was it. Rose wasn't sure about it. It certainly wasn't in the style of most craft beers today, which are normally labelled with some insufferably self-satisfied combination of street art overlaid with technical drawings and are named Hipster Dribble or some shit like that. Unicycle Oil. Martian Surf Diesel. It's too easy. Elizabethan Partridge Juice. There, I did it again.

When these great rolls of labels arrived a couple of weeks later, they were exactly as I had imagined. Next, I had to buy a labelling machine to apply the labels to the bottles. The automatic electric labelling machines start at about €3,000. However, I found an Italian-made manual labelling machine that worked with the turn of a handle for a few hundred euros, so I bought that and hoped for the best. It looked like something out of a Tim Burton film, but once I'd managed to fine-tune it to the dimensions of my bottles and labels, it was actually very effective.

Cantonese Owl Brine. Did it again.

On the face of it, making beer sounds like a good money-spinner. The main ingredients – malt, hops and yeast – are fairly cheap. It probably costs around fifty cents for the raw ingredients for one bottle of beer and you can sell it at the market round here for €2.50. That's a profit of 400 per cent. By the time the market came around, if there were no mishaps I would have 300 bottles of beer to sell. That was €750-worth!

But then you add in the cost of labels. When you are buying on a small scale like I am, your labels come out at thirty cents each. Bottles also come out at thirty cents each. Then you need bottle caps. You need a labelling machine to put the labels on. You need a professional bottle capper. Then there's all the electricity you use to brew the beer. Then there's the time it takes to get the beer from the fermenter into the bottles. Making beer takes five hours. Bottling it and labelling it takes days.

For your market stall you need tables, a gazebo, a banner, business cards, tasting cups, carrier boxes for people to take away their beer bottles and a cool box to keep your test beers cold. Most importantly, of course, you need branded aprons. A lot of this stuff was one-off purchases, but for Braslou market, even if I sold all my beer, I would still be well into the red. The beer venture was doomed. That was certain. But that wasn't the point now. The point was to wear branded aprons. And if the market went well, at least I might go out with a bit of glitter and a puff of smoke.

A week or so after meeting Claude Capaval I was sampling my latest beer in the barn. It wasn't going well. It was a flavour like licking a rusty tin can. It wasn't right, but I couldn't afford it not to be right. I could detect some good flavours in there, so that meant it was OK, didn't it? I could smell the citrus and the orange that came from the hops. I pretended it was OK. After all, this was the beer I had been trying to make all year. This brew had gone well. I had refined my recipe a tiny bit. This was the beer that I would sell at the market. I changed my mind. It was fine.

It wasn't fine and I didn't give it to Damien to try because, whether I was prepared to admit it or not, it wasn't fine at all, and he would tell me so much. I pretended it was fine.

I had begun brewing the day after Damien's exhibition, when we had decided to do the *marché de l'asperge*, but two weeks later, when I tasted the first batch at the bottling stage, it had an odd taste. Rather than risk bottling and wasting another two weeks, I ditched it and started again. I could afford to because I would still have time to make several hundred bottles of beer. But then the next batch I brewed tasted even worse. It was practically the same recipe as the beers I had taken to Damien and Celia's, but it tasted wrong. They were all wrong.

That evening I went to Fred the *vigneron*'s to get some wine. I often give him my beers to try and he is very enthusiastic.

The best thing about going to Fred's to buy wine is that it's not primarily a financial transaction. This is the case to a greater or lesser extent when you buy wine from any of the *vignerons* round here. With Fred it was more about tasting wine than selling wine, and it was a social occasion. The business side of things was secondary. I always bought the same thing from Fred and I had tasted all his wines before, but still he insisted on us tasting everything he had before any money changed hands.

It works like this: you go into his *cave*, which is full of fifteen-foot-tall cylindrical tanks, old cobwebbed bottles and oak barrels, he rinses a couple of dusty glasses off with the hosepipe curled up on the wall outside, and the tasting begins. You start with his white wine. Then his red wine. Then his sweet fizz. Then his dry fizz. Then you taste his white wine again. Then you have more fizz. Maybe a bottle. I try and say things I imagine people who know about wine saying, things like: 'It's got intricate tannins.'

Fred wears a forgiving smile. Then we try his white wine again. Then I might say, 'I like what you've done with the tannins.'

Then we'll try some *eau de vie* from an unmarked bottle and then anything else Fred can find. At some point he'll disappear off to the house and come back with some fresh melon that his wife Karine brought home from work. She runs a melon farm. Then we'll try more fizz. He only has four wines to try, but I am normally still there after two hours or more, leaning heavily on dangerous-looking wine-making machinery and blathering: 'What I like about this wine is the way its tannins are combining with its other tannins. It's a tannic harmony.' (Good name for a band.)

'Thanks,' deadpans Fred.

'Are these tannins different from the other tannins? What tannins did you use?'

'I don't . . . That's not how it works. They're just tannins.'

'TELL ME WHAT TANNINS YOU USE!'

What's most fantastic about Fred's wines is they taste of his *cave*. The old oak you can smell when you are at his *cave* is the same oak you can taste in his wine. I wanted my beer to be like that, to have this discernible link to it's origins, except our barn currently smelt of dry rot and mouse craps.

Once we've exhausted every available drop of wine, we'll try my beer, if I've brought some.

This time I gave him my latest bottle to try and immediately regretted it. As soon as he opened it, you could smell it wasn't right. Fred poured it. It was murky. It smelt bad. We tasted it together.

'I can't finish it,' said Fred. And from the look on his face he was being polite. He looked like he was on the verge of collapsing in on himself.

'OK, but it has good flavours too,' I said weakly. It was undrinkable. I knew it was. I had known this when I tried it as I bottled it two weeks before, but I couldn't admit it to myself. I had known this when I tried it earlier in the day. Ever since I had agreed to do the market my beers had become increasingly awful.

I could feel myself flushing red. Fred was one of my champions. Up until now he had been telling everyone in the village how good my beer was. Now what was he supposed to say?

Like a twelve-year-old who'd been dumped at the school disco, I fled. But first I drank another bottle or so of Fred's fizz before loading up the car with boxes of wine, tasting some more of Fred's red and finally heading home in shame after two more glasses of homemade fruit liqueur.

I couldn't sell this shit. I mean, it was a pointless exercise anyway. I told myself it didn't matter because the truth was, without a proper brewery the game was already up, regardless of whether this beer turned out well or not. But the thing was, I needed to sell something for me, just to show I could have done it if things had worked out differently. I needed a victory, but instead I was losing in bigger increments each time.

I started seriously contemplating returning to England in disgrace. Getting back into the rat race. I could already imagine the interview at the job centre: 'So, Mr Barnes, what skills do you have?'

'I'm good at thinking up shit band names.'

Portly, moustachioed men in tight nylon tops faded from a million washes, their synthetic fibres straining under the pressure of a lifetime of three-course lunches and sparkling under artificial light, stood facing each other as a cool March breeze wafted the scent of stale red wine around the pitch. This, ladies and gentlemen, was how we did football, Braslou veterans style. Try not to get aroused.

You have to be over thirty-five to qualify for the veterans' team, but there were players well into their fifties and even sixties playing. It was a Friday-night friendly match. Maybe that was why most of them had been in the bars since the early afternoon, although I suspect they'd have done the same had it been the World Cup final.

I was a relative youngster here. I thought perhaps that for the first time in my life I would be one of the faster players on the pitch, but it turned out that most of the players, even the older men, were more than a match for me.

Nevertheless, it was one of the most enjoyable matches I'd played. When you're young there's always a slightly threatening atmosphere on a football pitch. Now, I don't want to start disparaging young people, but in general, they are hell-bent on mindless violence. Actually, even in veterans' teams it's impossible to have twenty-two men playing football without one psychopath going round kick-ing people: it is a medical fact that one in twenty-two men has a homicidal urge to kick people in the legs as hard as he possibly can. But luckily, in this case, he was on my side. Generally, it was played in a really good spirit. Competitive enough to make it interesting but with one eye firmly on getting comprehensively banjoed afterwards.

I had hardly played football all season, but I just needed something to lift me from the durge. Having a baby in a foreign country away from the support of your family and friends is tough enough. We'd had visits from our family that were always a welcome relief, but for the most part of the last six months it had been just me, Rose and Albert, who was now ten months old, battling through. Once the summer had died away we'd been imprisoned in the living room, huddling round the log burner to keep warm. Looking back, there was so much pressure on us. I mean, we knew a few people; we had Damien and Celia, but they had their own baby to look after. We saw less and less of them as the year wore on.

Then there was our economic situation. Our finances were desperate, the brewery plan was in tatters, but we carried on. The three of us in that room. Nothing was being solved, nothing productive was happening, and we were starting to hear horror stories about getting thrown out of France because of Brexit, an event we'd almost completely missed at the time because we had a one-week-old baby. What's more, my nan's alarm clock had started haunting me again, but now all it displayed were four red zeros, flashing alarmingly, and even worse, I was having dreams about living in Aunty Maggs's house, watching the cliff erode from the kitchen window. The only positive about that time was that being so tired meant it was difficult to focus on anything other than the immediate: gardening, washing bottles, changing nappies, feeding, so that we never really got a chance to stare over the cliff.

But just when it felt like we'd reached breaking point, things changed for the better. It's amazing how much one's mood is affected by the seasons. Now it was March and when the sun pushed through you could actually feel the warmth of it. The log burner was only lit in the evenings. The stand at the asparagus market gave me something to aim for, as long as I could work out how to fix my beer. Best of all, at the start of March Albert started spending three days a week with a *nounou*. A *nounou* is a sort of nanny, although it sounds more like a witch doctor to me. This meant a great lifting of pressure. It was impossible to get anything done with a baby around, so all of a sudden we were free to get on with things for half the week. The *nounou* was Damien's mum, Annie. Annie might be the most remarkable person I've ever met. She looks after several children from the ages of six months up to four or five years old. Her first children are dropped off at 6 a.m. and her last child leaves at 6 p.m. Trying to look after one baby took absolutely everything that we had, yet Annie effortlessly marshalled a gang of kids, who would normally be intent on eating superglue and sticking their fingers in plugs, with consummate ease. She had turned it into an art form.

Albert would cry when we left him at Annie's, but by the time you picked him up he wouldn't want to leave. He rapidly formed some kind of deep criminal bond with Zoe, who also stayed there.

This is probably not what you're supposed to say about your children – I mean, you love them more than anything, etc., and all those other things that people say about their children – but suddenly having three days a week away from your child is absolutely bloody fantastic. I mean, it is really wonderful not to be in the company of your child all the time. It's heaven. People don't say that enough. It was just the fillip I needed.

At around the same time we brought in Madame Maciet to help round the house once a week. It was the time-saving equivalent of signing Lionel Messi. Madame Maciet was an absolute house-cleaning machine. In her early fifties, no nonsense, all action, she would turn up in her *sans permis,* a little car about half as long and two thirds as wide as a Mini, puffing out a distinct whiff of burning plastic as it squealed to a halt. *Sans permis* are these little cars with an engine so small you don't need a driving licence to drive them. They're a phenomenon in France. If you don't have a licence you can buy one of these and buzz around the place at 45 kph per hour. More importantly perhaps, if you've been banned for speeding or drink driving, you can hop in a *sans permis* and you're mobile again (I'd like to make it

111

clear this was not why Madame Maciet had one). They are almost always held together with gaffer tape, to the point that I wonder if they come out of the factory like that. At the end of the production line there's just some guy gaffer-taping any bits that look like they are flapping around.

Madame Maciet would march into the house, slam back a short black coffee, give a mesmerised Albert a big kiss on the forehead and then plough through the house, putting everything in order, before finishing every day without fail by slamming back a well-earned beer, and off she'd go in the little *sans permis*. Rose and I were both working as much as we could, but until now trying to keep a baby alive and a house from descending into chaos was taking up much too much of our time. Madame Maciet and Annie the *nounou* changed that.

It's very easy for beer to get contaminated, as it turns out. Any sort of bacteria or wild yeast that happens to be float-ing by can potentially ruin your beer. Haunted once again by my nan's alarm clock, I spent sleepless nights reading beer-related internet forums in order to understand why my latest brews weren't working, and the more I read, the more I realised that the most likely reason was they'd been infected in some way. That was why they were so acrid. It wasn't at all surprising, when I thought about it. The way I brewed was haphazard. Bits of equipment hadn't been cleaned for weeks. Other bits lay on the floor of the barn, where at night they were probably being used as some kind of sex playground for rats. Great swathes of rats doing it all night on my bloody siphoning equipment. When I pictured it in my head, I was furious with them. All these rats dressed in leather and chains hammering away at each other on my wort cooler. But leaving equipment lying around like that – it was just how I did things. I had always done it. *Why do more than the minimum?* I always thought. *It's not efficient to do more than the minimum.*

I was helping Monsieur Richard out in his hallowed vegetable garden when I realised how I could fix my beer: I had to change. We were digging a drainage canal to better irrigate the garden. How it could have been any better irrigated I wasn't really sure, but that was classic Monsieur Richard – he stopped at nothing in his pursuit of excellence. I was watching him meticulously cleaning his garden tools when a conversation he'd had with Rose a few months before jumped into my mind.

'Don't you have problems with slugs and snails eating your vegetables?' she'd asked.

'No,' replied Monsieur Richard. 'It's like anything in life. If it is *propre* – you maintain it and keep it clean from weeds – it takes care of itself.'

And suddenly I understood exactly what he meant. Like everything I had done previously in my life, I had been doing the minimum possible when brewing – taking shortcuts, cheating wherever I could – and now, as always happened, I was paying the price. It may have been bacteria specifically that was ruining my beer, but the overall reason for the beer being bad was the simple fact that I was cutting corners. The same reason why I didn't really prosper as a graphic designer in London. The same reason why I didn't become the lead guitarist for a rock band that brought 1980s hair metal back to the masses. I just couldn't be bothered to do things properly. The brewery equipment had become contaminated because I was trying to cheat. I wasn't cleaning down with enough effort. I was leaving jobs half finished. Monsieur Richard's gardening equipment was more sanitary than my beer-making equipment.

As I watched Monsieur Richard work, I realised he never does the minimum. He does as much as he possibly can. He doesn't buy cheap equipment that will just do. He gets the best quality equipment. He doesn't chuck his vegetables in the ground and hope that some will grow out of the mess. He takes the extra time. He plants them at the right depth, with the right spacing. He doesn't just spray a bit of water at them from a hosepipe. He has created an entire watering system that runs through his vegetable patch to make sure all the vegetables are watered properly. He doesn't leave his equipment out on the floor in the rain. He cleans everything down and stores it away properly.

And I began to understand as I watched him that the problem with only doing the bare minimum is that you might get away with it for a time, but sooner or later you'll get behind. There'll be a time when you can't do the minimum, maybe you haven't the time that day, or your idiot hound has broken into the back field and has got his head stuck in the neighbour's chicken wire again, so you have to go and deal with that scenario, and because of this you find that you can't do what you needed to do. That's when you start getting behind, and that's when you start running into trouble. Because Monsieur Richard always does the maximum he possibly can, if he gets caught out then he's still ahead. He's got plenty in the bank. He can cover any mishaps or mistakes.

I had to be more like Monsieur Richard if I wanted my beer to succeed. I think I had known that for a while, but seeing him in action really brought it home. If I was selling beer to the public, I had to make sure it was *propre*, not just for me, but for them. Even if they were pricks. I had to start making everything *propre*. No more shortcuts. I would start doing everything properly, I would do more than I needed to, and whenever I was tempted to do a half-arsed job I would say to myself, *What would Monsieur Richard do?* And a picture of him flying off into the sunset on his gleaming ride-on lawnmower would appear in my mind.

Mincing around our barn, one finger to my mouth like I was Hercule Poirot about to give it the big reveal, I scrutinised all my pieces of equipment. After not more than four minutes of mincing, I decided the most likely source of contamination was the big plastic fermenter, because the beer was being spoilt each time, and plastic fermenters can be tricky. The problem is, unlike steel fermenters, it's easy to accidentally scratch the surface of plastic fermenters, and if you do this it gives a potential hiding place for bacteria, so that no matter how many times you clean it, you never get rid of the bacteria and your beer is spoilt each time.

I gave everything a thorough clean for the first time in about a year and I binned my old fermenters and ordered three new ones, vowing to no one in particular that I would brew three more beers. If these final efforts came out as badly as the last few, I told myself, I would give up on brewing beer altogether and concentrate on doing more gardening work, and, make no mistake, I knew what this really meant: one day as the misery became too much to bear, I would throw myself under a ride-on lawnmower, which would immediately cut out, as they have sensors on their seats so if you fall off, they stop, so I would have to pick myself up, hope no one saw, and carry on gardening, miserable for the rest of my life, my only company being an apparition of an old alarm clock that basically only appeared when I was about to fuck everything up.

The thing about my nan's alarm clock is that I purposely introduced it into my psyche so, really, I only have myself to blame that it haunts me now. I've always been the type of person who is unwilling to face their problems. If there is a credit-card bill that I can't afford, I won't try and find some solution, I'll just ignore it. I'll stop opening the letters from the credit-card company. My nan, a tough little woman from the East End of London who was a firefighter during the war and smoked cigarettes with such regularity that it seemed she used them as a necessary protection against the damaging effects of clean air, saw this trait in me early on and took it upon herself to try and turn me round. When we travelled over to her flat at the top of a '60s tower block in Bethnal Green on a Sunday for roast dinner and ciga-rette fumes, she would lecture me on the need to face one's problems at all costs.

'You've got to face up to life,' she'd say.

'OK, Nan. I'll definitely do that,' I'd lie.

I ignored her advice for a long time, but when she died I began to think more seriously about what she had been trying to tell me and I realised that ignoring my problems was not producing the results I hoped it would. So, when-ever I got in this sort of situation where I was hiding from the truth, I began imagining my nan's alarm clock count-ing down and at the end of the countdown, normally ten seconds, I would force myself to face whatever the problem was. It didn't always help. The older you get the harder it is to break habits, but that was how it originally started. It was a mechanism to help me face up to life. But then the clock went rogue.

BEER NO. 7:

Enslaved Elf Munich Ale

RECIPE	MISTAKES
4.2 kg Pale malt	Too much Munich malt
2 kg Munich malt	Attempting to imitate
10 g Nugget hops at 90 minutes	an articulated lorry
20 g Citra at 10 minutes	
50 g Citra dry hops in the fermenter	

We British are much closer to the French than we think we are, but there are some subtle but none-theless fundamental philosophical ways in which we differ. Namely, traffic roundabouts. A Briton approaches a round-about expecting another car to be coming and therefore slows down. A French person approaches a roundabout in the same way that Evel Knievel approached a jump – any loss of speed is seen as potentially catastrophic. The French view is that if everybody arrives at the roundabout at the same speed and as long as there's no one directly in front of you, then everyone can pass round the roundabout successfully and at a thrilling speed. And when it works, it's a much more efficient system than the British one. There's virtually no loss of time and you save on brake pads. Of course, if there is someone in front of you when you hit the roundabout, then you crash into them. But you just give a simple Gallic shrug as you pull them out of the wreckage and everyone is on their way, happy as can be.

Road markings are taken as a polite suggestion in France. A suggestion that is widely ignored in favour of driving the perfect racing line. I believe this is a major part of the syllabus of their driving lessons and has been for many years, for it is not just the boy racers who pursue the perfect racing line, it is drivers of all ages and sexes. I have several times been forced to swerve onto the grass verge to avoid elderly French farmers' wives in tiny little cars coming round the bend in the opposite lane, their faces set in grim concentration, intent on hitting the apex of the bend even if that means having all four wheels on my side of the white lines. At least, they would have all four wheels on my side of the white lines if two of them weren't off the ground.

And while we're on the subject of grass verges, in France they are as much a part of the road as, well, the road. On a narrow road, you don't slow down to let someone else through, you simply both drive up the grass verges on either side without ever taking your foot off the accelerator. In fact, losing speed in most situations is a big no-no.

I try to drive like the French now. It's a lot more fun. Every approach to a roundabout is death or glory. What a way to live each day! You might think that the French are terrible drivers, but on the contrary, they are much better than the British, and that is why they can get away with driving like Red Bull-soaked ferrets. On motorways,

British drivers will quite often plod along in the middle lane even when there's plenty of room in the slow lane, too scared to pull in, and too scared to overtake in the fast lane. The French don't do this. They always pull into the slow lane if there's space, but equally they are more than happy to hurtle down the fast lane like thunderbolts. Because of this, their motorways run much more efficiently. When they are overtaking in the fast lane they leave their indicators on. It's wonderfully liberating: you really should try it. I do it all the time now. I hammer the accelerator down on the 1999 Renault Mégane estate, an action that has almost no noticeable effect, and then I cruise down the fast lane with my indicator on, thinking of champagne and scantily clad women. That, my friends, is how to fucking drive.

It helps that there are fewer people on the roads over here. The UK is the tenth most gridlocked country in the world. Last time I drove in England I got off the ferry in Portsmouth and sat in a traffic jam all the way to London. It horrifies me that people do that every day. They must be completely insane.

Driving is far more aggressive in England. All that repressed sexual tension manifests itself as angry driving. Every white-van driver who cuts you up is essentially shouting to the world, 'I HAVE A MICRO-PENIS AND I WANT TO FEEL THE DELICIOUS CRACK OF A WHIP WIELDED BY AN OBESE WOMAN NAMED JANET AGAINST MY LATEX-COVERED BUTTOCKS WHILST HANGING FROM MY ANKLES OVER THE SIDE OF A FISHING BOAT, MY HEAD DRAGGING THROUGH A SWARM OF HORNY JELLYFISH!' In France, driving is a relaxing

119

experience. In Britain it's like getting caught in an English Defence League rally. Men who commit road-rage offences in England should be sentenced to a month in the fishnet stockings that they have secretly wanted to wear since an eye-opening school trip to see *Cabaret* the musical as a thirteen-year-old. I believe it would help them relax.

The only really stressful thing about driving in France is that, if you are driving in the countryside, even if there is no one around for miles, within seconds you will find a white Peugeot hatchback right up your arse, metaphorically speaking. It's an unexplainable phenomenon, so it's best just to get on with things and not think about it too much.

I was planning a road trip. A short one, admittedly – two hours to be exact – but it still counted. It was time for a trip to the malt house in the mythical town of Issoudun.

Up until now I had been buying English and Belgian malts from the internet. It wasn't a cost-effective way of buying malt, especially the quantities I needed for the market. Xavier had told me about the malt house in Issoudun, a town a couple of hours' drive away, where I could get French malts at a much cheaper price. You had to buy in bulk, though. Issoudun sounded like a town from *Lord of the Rings*. A great Elfen civilisation. A mystical, beautiful citadel of delicate towers and temples.

I hopped into the 1999 Renault Mégane estate, admired for a moment the passionate roar of the 1.8-litre engine and blasted out of our great iron gates. Immediately I knew something was wrong. It felt like one of the wheels was dragging along the tarmac. I stuck my head out of my window to see what was happening. One of the wheels was dragging along the tarmac. This didn't stop me from bravely ploughing on for a hundred metres until the squealing sound became too much and I pulled onto the grass verge and sat for a while in silence.

After ten minutes or so, Damien pulled up in his giant white truck. Colleen was in the passenger seat. She waved excitedly.

'What's the problem?' asked Damien.

'Oh, you know. I reckon it's the brake cords. The brake pulleys, maybe.' It's important to try and pretend to know about man things when talking to other men.

'The wheel is locked. It may be the brake disc,' said Damien.

'Yeah, the brake disc. I thought the same. That or the brake socks.'

'I'll tow you round the corner so you're off the road and you can get a breakdown recovery truck to pick it up from there.'

'Thanks, Damien. Ruddy brake lanterns, eh? I hear they are a common problem in the old Renault Méganes.'

After Damien had gone, I ran back to our house, leaving the 1999 Renault Mégane beached on the verge, and hopped into the 2007 Renault Grand Scénic, our other car. We'd bought it several months after moving to Braslou from a local butcher. I try and avoid talking about it because I'm ashamed of it. It's a sort of tall, rounded box of a toy car made for all the family. This wasn't ideal. At least the 1999 Renault Mégane estate was vaguely utilitarian. The Scénic was the least masculine of all cars. It was not designed for carrying large sacks of malt. It was designed for pushchairs and dribbling children. It had compartments in the floor to hide used nappies and trays to wipe bogies on. It did not have suspension designed to take a quarter of a tonne of malt. Nevertheless, off I drove to Issoudun in the 2007

Renault Scénic, my trusty hound Burt at my side glaring at me, as ever, like I'd just pushed his grandmother down a lift shaft.

From Braslou you drive almost directly east for two hours, going through elegant, tuffeau- built, château-studded towns and villages woven together with rivers and streams. But then, as you approach Issoudun, rather than towers chiselled from some magical sparkling marble stone by slender Elfen hands to create architecture so detailed, wondrous and beautiful that it was almost beyond the comprehension of human kind, as I'd anticipated, a monstrous brown fortress lumbers onto the horizon. A concrete fortress so dour that even in the bright sunshine it sucks in all the light and happiness in the world and takes a great big shit on it. This brown fortress that polluted the landscape for miles around was the malt house. For some reason I felt guilty about this, like I was complicit.

We pulled up to the malt house: me, nervous and excited, and Burt desperate for a crap. It was a vast 1970s complex of concrete buildings that must have covered four or five acres and, as we followed the signs to the pick-up area, we were cast into shadow by huge articulated lorries that rumbled around us, threatening to squash us flat. They had arrived to collect hundreds and thousands of tonnes of malt for the mega-breweries that pump out litres of Kronenbourg and Heineken by the million. The staff at the warehouse were surprised then when I backed into the loading bay in the stupid family-friendly Renault Scénic. How they laughed, the men in lorries and the men working in the warehouse, as I made my own beeping noises while I reversed, in an attempt to be accepted as one of them. Oh, how they laughed as I arranged sacks of malt like passengers across the back seat and strapped them in with seat belts to balance the weight. Yes, they laughed, but I could sense a tangible feeling of admiration. Extremely well-disguised admiration, almost undetectable to the untrained eye. The most uplifting sort of admiration – admiration masked by loud, mocking laughter. Throughout this ordeal I could only think of one thing: what had they done with the elves?

I got the malt home, though. The rear bumper of the Scénic was practically dragging along the road, but I got it home. No more buying ingredients here and there from the internet. That was for home brewers. This was malt on a commercial scale. What I really needed was a brewery big enough to match it.

'It's too bitter,' said Damien.

'Goddammit. Rusted fucking sardine cans full of sawdust on thin little wheels made by drunken, stripey-jumpered, garlic-necklaced, arrogant twats.'

'What did you say?'

'I said it's supposed to be a little bitter, Damien.'

'Well, it's too bitter, but it's nice. The best yet. Have you thought about making a blonde beer?'

We were sitting in Damien's yard, looking past the field inhabited by their horses, Fanny and Applejack, towards the Richelieu Forest and we were trying my latest IPA. The beer had been healed. I had known that when I tasted it before bottling, a couple of weeks ago, but I didn't want to jinx it. It had come out well and I was overjoyed. Relieved and overjoyed. The clean-down had worked. I was more like Monsieur Richard and I felt like a king. This must be how he felt all the time. This was a beer that could be sold at the market.

The IPA was my best beer so far. It was a little bit darker than I wanted (I was hoping for a red beer, but this was brown), but using darker malts had, I think, lowered the pH of the mash, which meant that the hop flavours were smoother and less acrid. I'd also added marbles to the bag of hops when dry hopping it, to make the hops sink into the beer, because otherwise they tend to just float on the top of the liquid. Sinking them meant that they had had more contact with the beer and imparted more flavour.

I was dry hopping with Cascade and Mandarina Bavaria hops. Cascade is the classic American IPA hop: piney and citrusy. But my beer was moving away from the classic American IPA. The Cascade hops I used were grown in Alscace in eastern France and, just like wine grapes, hops grown in different regions, in different soils, have different characters, so in the same way that a New Zealand Pinot Noir isn't the same as a Burgundian Pinot Noir, my Cascade wasn't quite the same as American Cascade. It was greener, more lemony. Mandarina Bavaria hops, a relatively new variety from Germany, gave it orangey notes. They worked well with the Cascade. Not only this, the beer wasn't pale any more. I had started out using only pale ale malt, but over time, as I'd tried to get the pH baIance right, I'd introduced darker malts like Munich malt and Crystal malt, and even roasted barley, which is traditionally used in stout, and so my beer had a richer, more complex malt quality. I wasn't sure if it was an IPA any more; it certainly wasn't just a pale imitation of Big Job, and I was pleased about this. I had made a beer that was its own thing, and that thing wasn't revolting. I don't know how this beer would have stood up to other commercial beers, but it was honest, drinkable beer. Beer I could sell.

By the time the market came around, I would have around 300 bottles of beer, as long as the other batches that were still fermenting turned out OK.

'Animals can sense if you're uptight. I once got within a metre of a wild peahen,' said Claude, Damien's dad, in a way that meant I was supposed to be impressed. And, consequently, I was impressed, although I didn't know why. Claude occupies a higher state of being. I was very impressed. He looks like Damien, but he's more ethereal and he's less hell-bent on getting things done all the time. He arrives in waves and he disappears in a moment. When Claude speaks, you can't help but take notice.

People often ask me if I have a plan for the brewery. I normally fob them off with something about third-quarter growth and the guy who invented the plastic bits on the end of laces and now he makes the wings of space shuttles or the water jets in bidets or something. I don't know. I didn't have a plan, of course. Not past knowing that I had to make beer and then I had to sell it to make sure my family didn't starve. I hadn't written a single number on a piece of paper. I was talking to Claude about the brewery. Claude didn't ask me if I had a plan. He knew I didn't. He said this: 'Don't try and get rich. That's the most important thing. Build your business slowly. Start by selling beer in a fifty-kilometre radius. Markets, bars, shops. Then after two years, if it's going well, expand by another fifty kilometres and so on. But, most importantly, remember to live. Don't try and get rich and forget to live.'

This was a plan I could follow. I loved Claude for this advice and I recited it to myself whenever I was in danger of working too hard and not drinking enough wine. Come to think of it, I'm not sure that situation ever occurred, but I remained vigilant. In all the time I lived in the UK, nobody ever said that to me. It was always *Work as hard as you can and earn as much as you can.* I didn't do that, of course. I was much more naturally suited to Claude's advice.

I thought if I took what I learnt from Monsieur Richard and combined It with Claude's advice I would probably be somewhere close to living a good life. Do what you do to the best standard you can, but don't kill yourself working.

For the asparagus market I only had my red IPA-style beer, but I had been developing a porter as well. Nobody agrees on what makes a porter different from a stout. Some people say a stout is different from a porter because it uses roasted barley, but others say that this is not it at all and a stout is just a type of porter with something extra to it – more alcohol, or more hops. I couldn't give a shit either way. My porter was coming out better and better. I didn't bother brewing any for the asparagus market because I thought it probably wouldn't be the sort of beer people would want, but actually, when I gave it to the people round here it generally got a good reception. I dry hopped it with a little bit of Mandarina Bavaria to get a chocolate-orange flavour.

Burt had started digging holes in the garden. I thought perhaps there was some root vegetable that he had discovered, or there was a burrowing animal that he was trying to catch, but after a week or so I came to the depressing realisation, based on the placing and size of the holes, that he was trying to booby-trap the garden so that I might trip and fall on my face. No amount of punishment dissuaded him from digging holes. He was like this with everything. He would just carry on doing whatever it was he wanted to do. People who meet Burt often come to the erroneous conclusion that he's an idiot. That he's too stupid to realise the consequences of his actions. Too dense to be trained. I wondered the same thing for quite a while, before concluding that that is exactly what he wants you to think. We are, in fact, the idiots and Burt knows only too well what he's doing. He's trying to destroy humanity, one despicable act after the other. That's what he's doing.

He lives in a different universe. Not a universe with different values, but a universe where values as we understand them don't exist. There's no logic to his actions. Instead, some other system completely unfathomable to people of our universe presides. I'm not talking about a universe of dog values – Louis, his brother, is equally as perplexed by Burt as I am. No, Burt is the *other*.

I talk a lot about Burt because he's this kind of great evil that follows me wherever I go, but by now you're probably wondering what had happened to Louis. Louis' story was a terrible one. Even now, when I think of what happened that fateful day, 3 April 2017, I shudder.

Louis was a kind, thoughtful and well-behaved dog. Consequently, he didn't get anywhere near as much attention as Burt. Louis' story, more than anything, highlights the plain unfairness of life.

When we called the dogs in, Louis was always first there. Burt only came if he got a treat. You didn't have to bribe Louis to not be an arsehole. You did have to bribe Burt. This meant that Burt was constantly being rewarded for doing what he should have been doing anyway. Burt got all the treats.

We should have seen it coming, really. No one can endure that injustice forever. No one can watch such a despicable creature as Burt winning in life, when he does everything wrong. No one can watch their perfect behaviour go unrewarded time after time while their brother deliberately fucks everything up over and over again and is rewarded handsomely. No, even for a creature as good-natured as Louis, the injustice became too much to bear. So we come to 3 April.

We'd been for our daily family outing to the *hypermarché* in Chinon. Even after living in France for over a year, the exotic allure of a French supermarket had not waned. They still sell horsemeat in French supermarkets – what a riot! We'd even stayed for lunch. Treated ourselves to an excellent three-course meal of endive salads and confit duck legs in the supermarket restaurant. You don't get that in Tesco. Then we returned home, not imagining in the slightest what an utterly dreadful scene awaited us. You see, that morning, before we left, we'd called the dogs into the kitchen. We normally leave them in the kitchen if we are going to be away for a few hours – we'd stopped electrocuting them due to the rising cost of electricity bills, and we couldn't leave them outside for too long, as they might eat the chickens or escape to Paris or be radicalised by fundamentalist terrorists. The problem was, while Louis returned to the kitchen immediately, as is the norm, Burt refused to come, deciding instead to continue his search for some kind of major power cord to chew in the undergrowth. We should have persisted in trying to get him in. We should have bribed him, but in the end we thought, 'Ah sod it. We'll keep Louis in the kitchen and we'll leave Burt in the garden because he's an arsehole.' We weren't too worried about Burt being out in the garden on his own because Burt, for all his bravado, is a follower, not a leader. He generally won't go anywhere if Louis hasn't gone there first, so we thought he probably wouldn't try and escape. This was grossly unfair to Louis of course, who, as usual, had done exactly what we had asked and because of that had been imprisoned in a tiny kitchen while Burt roamed free in the sun. And that, simply, was once too much for Louis.

Something was wrong when we returned to the house. Burt was standing outside the kitchen door, whimpering. Through the window I could see the bin had been knocked over. Used nappies were torn and shredded on the floor. Even more alarmingly, hundreds of chewed Nespresso capsules were strewn across the kitchen. I had been saving them to recycle, but that morning Burt had chewed my car door and Gadget had bitten me on the knee and at that point I had decided that the universe would be better off if we stopped recycling things and left the earth to turn into a fireball, so I'd chucked a big bag of the Nespresso capsules into the bin. And now it appeared Louis had eaten them all.

I feared the worst. We entered the kitchen and picked our way through the debris. Burt stayed outside, still whimpering. Louis was nowhere to be seen. The door from the kitchen to the living room had been forced open.

We tiptoed through the house, not knowing what we would find. After a quick search it became clear that Louis wasn't on the ground floor. Rose pointed to the ceiling and mouthed 'upstairs' like a commando would. The thing is, Louis wasn't allowed upstairs. He'd never been upstairs, he'd never before showed the slightest interest in going upstairs, and yet he wasn't downstairs, so now he must be upstairs. This was unnerving. Tiptoeing upstairs to the landing, we were both hit by a dreadful smell. A quick check of the nursery and the study proved fruitless. That left one room – our bedroom. As any hero would, I told Rose to step back while I entered. I thought I was prepared for anything, but I wasn't prepared for what I saw.

'Oh, dear God, Rose.'

'Is he dead?' Rose said.

I couldn't answer. There, lying prostrate across the floor of the bedroom, was an enormous shit. A monstrous turd on the rug. Meanwhile Louis, jacked up on Nespresso capsules, his eyes bulging – I'm not shitting you, I could see them pulsing – lapped the room at the most extraordinary speed like a mechanical hare, ploughing through his own poo over and over again, leaving a trail of it around the edge of the bedroom.

It's something I hope I never have to witness again and it's a lesson for us all. Don't take the good guys for granted, because if you do, eventually they'll shit in your bedroom.

It took several days for Louis to return to normal. He had made his point. Now he gets more treats.

Two chickens arrived. I assumed it was to do with Rose's pregnancy cravings, which was really too confusing because it was now almost a year since she'd given birth.

The night before the *marché de l'asperge,* a clear night, a night of a billion stars and other space matter, we packed up Damien's van full of beer and branded aprons. It was going to be an early start. I was nervous.

Market day. Picture this: an ochre sun climbs through streaks of purple cloud that stretch to the horizon and beyond. The fresh morning air is cool and clear. All around, bare-chested men go about their business. Men's men. Men's men's men. Also some women. Possibly women's women. I don't know what that means, but they sound alluring and likely to work in the trades. Everywhere people are preparing for an event that is of incredible significance. The atmosphere is primed, coiled with anticipation. Then from the depths of hell great engines roar and in the background an inspiring guitar-led soft-rock soundtrack plays. What I have just described is the opening credits to Tom Cruise's art-house film *Days of Thunder*, but the scene that surrounded us as we set up our stall at the Braslou *marché de l'asperge* reminded me of it a great deal. Other stallholders seemed underwhelmed by the occasion.

The day started badly. Some of Rose's family were staying for the weekend and the night before, driven by a mixture of childlike curiosity and an unquenchable thirst for knowledge as all the best scientists are, my brother-in-law Arthur and I decided to try and drink a magnum of cheap red wine each, as fast as we possibly could. The results were spectacular: I have never been so animated about an episode of whatever that show is called where Michael Portillo makes endless fucking train journeys, but at 6 a.m. the next day, as I fumbled around in a faraway state, trying to put pants on my head while brushing my teeth with a candlestick, I almost regretted it.

It got worse. When we arrived at the market, Damien parked up the van and went to find out where our stand was. He called me on the mobile a few minutes later, telling me to drive the van to the other end of the road. Excited at the chance of driving a van, and hence moving one step closer to my dream of producing some small amount of testosterone, I began the task of trying to get it out of the parking space. There were stalls set up all around us and vans unloading front and back. It would require a tricky manoeuvre. A tricky manoeuvre for your average driver, but I comforted myself that I had superior spatial awareness.

Seven minutes of frantically turning the steering wheel and driving backwards and forwards and finding myself in exactly the same position ensued. It was a problem completely impossible for my red wine-gunked brain to solve. It must have been the most pathetic attempt at getting out of a car-parking space ever witnessed. And it was witnessed. Most of the other market-stall owners had by now gathered to watch with incredulity as I over-revved the engine and rolled two inches forward and then two inches back for the thirtieth time, until finally the man with the vegetable stall opposite tapped on the window, shook his head and gruffly signalled me to get out, like a trainer throwing in the towel for his punch-drunk fighter. He got in and, after performing a couple of fairly routine manoeuvres, reversed it out of the space and down the road in under three seconds. Then he got out and walked off without even looking at me.

I was already flustered, then Damien asked me to tie our banner to the stand. A tricky task for your average punter, but not for someone who had mastered the overhand knot to the degree I had. Seven minutes of huffing later, a small crowd had gathered. The same crowd, I rather suspect. By now I was feeling the force of a most extraordinary red-wine hangover. Finally, Damien took over.

'Enough of these English knots. I will do a French knot.'

The *marché de l'asperge* was set along the main road that runs through Braslou, from Richelieu to Marigny-Marmande.

132

It's a straight road flanked by modest old houses in tuffeau, some rendered in sandy white, which huddle together as you get towards the middle of the village. At the start of the village there was a marquee set up for the special lunch (at most of these fêtes they have a large sit-down lunch to celebrate whatever it is they are celebrating) and a couple of booze stands along the way. Most of the people there were selling asparagus, but there were other stalls as well. Fruit and veg stalls, pasta stalls, plants, wine.

There isn't much in Braslou. The smallest *mairie* or town hall in the region, Bruno's restaurant and bar, and that's pretty much it. There used to be much more. Damien can remember when there were four or five bars, a *boulangerie*, a butcher and a general store. Damien is in his late twenties, so if he can remember it, the decline must have happened quite quickly. Sadly, this is typical of rural France. A combination of the rise of supermarkets on the edge of towns, the fall in the profitability of agriculture and the increasing lure of big towns and cities for young people means that the economic climate for a small shop in a small village is perilous.

And yet something seems to be happening in Braslou. There are young families moving in. Houses are being built. Somebody constructed a par-three golf course on the outskirts. That is bloody madness in an area like this, but he/she could sense it. There is a seed. An industrial zone on the outskirts that has several flourishing businesses. Sylvain, a young man from the village who had a stall next to mine at the market, had just started an enterprise making artisanal pasta. Artisanal pasta is not the sign of a village in decline.

The market began without me realising it. Before we'd

even got a chance to put our branded aprons on. I don't know quite what I was expecting, some kind of klaxon to signify that it had started, or perhaps Dale Winton hang-gliding in to cut a ribbon, but instead, as we were finishing our set-up, people started wandering up and down the street.

No one stopped at our stall. People glanced and laughed, but no one stopped. I hadn't appreciated quite how personal selling something that you had made is. It was me out there behind the table and if no one bought anything, it would be a humiliation. I'd be the laughing stock of the village. And worse, it would be the same for Damien too. He'd stood up alongside the funny little Englishman, but whereas I didn't really have a reputation to lose because I wasn't very well known round here, he was, and he did. Then Monsieur Richard arrived.

'Bonjour Tommy, how's it going?'

'Yeah, good. A bit slow, but I'm sure it will pick up.'

'Yes, don't worry. I will buy twelve bottles of beer.'

Our first sale! He handed over €24 and I gave him the beer and it was as simple as that. Now, I know for a fact that Monsieur Richard didn't really like my beer. And that's all right. It's not to everyone's tastes. He liked blonde beers. Beers that quench the thirst. Not my dark, mysterious hoppy, heavy beers. I had long ago stopped giving him bottles of my beer to try because I knew he was running out of polite ways to say he didn't like it. But that was the person he was. He saw a man dying on his arse in a foreign land, and he stepped in and bought twelve bloody beers that he didn't even want, and I will be forever in debt to him for that. Because all of a sudden other people came to the stall. They had seen Monsieur

Richard buying beer and, whether they knew him or not – and most people probably did – they had taken one look at him and thought, *That is a man who has mastered life. If he is buying beer, then I will buy beer.* Because that is the power that Monsieur Richard has. And suddenly we were inundated.

Damien's claim to know everyone in the village turned out to be true, as he called passer-by after passer-by over to try the beer. The stock began flying out of the boxes.

Customers came to chat. They wanted to know how the beer was made, what was in it. I told them all the processes you go through to make beer; I bored on about malts and hops and how they affected the flavour. Alongside me, Damien didn't know what was in the beer, so he was making up all that stuff – I mean, he was saying literally any old shit, but it didn't matter, it was working. As more and more people came to our stall, we couldn't keep up. We weren't at all prepared for this level of interest; we were swamped and things were starting to go awry. People were receiving the wrong change, customers were waiting and getting irate, when from nowhere Claude, Damien's dad, appeared behind the bar next to us and started serving customers, and his presence alone calmed everyone. By 10.30 a.m. things had died down, largely because we had sold out. Three hundred bottles in an hour and a half. People from the village were asking for the empty bottles to take as a souvenir. It was overwhelming. I turned to Claude to thank him, but he had gone. Disappeared like a guardian angel. Vanished into thin air. Or possibly the wine tent.

The market didn't finish till 2 p.m. and we couldn't get the van in to pack up before then, so the only thing we could do was to celebrate at Bruno's bar for the rest of the morning. People came and chatted to us. People made orders for beer. People wanted to visit the brewery. At some point the local newspaper reporter asked if he could come to the house and do an interview in the week. Friends passed by to to say hello. Nick and Claire, Fred the *vigneron*, Celia, Colleen and Zoe. Members of the Braslou football team stopped to see how we were doing – Charlus, Jonathan and many more. We had succeeded in a way that I never thought we could.

In the excitement of the market (by which I mean I was drunk), I'd forgotten about the journalist's visit altogether, so it took me by surprise when he turned up a few days later. He asked a few questions about the brewery and what my plans were, he tried a couple of the beers and took a couple of photos, which was slightly embarrassing because the day before I had managed to get incredibly sunburnt, so I had a big red tomato head. I didn't think he really had enough to make an article, so I thought nothing of it.

The following week I spotted my giant tomato head splashed across the pages of the local newspaper alongside an article full of quotes that I don't remember saying but that made me sound clever and like I'd had a plan all along. It was fantastic publicity. People stopped me in the street to talk about beer and remark on my giant tomato head. The article included my phone number and on the back of it I began getting several people a day phoning me asking to buy beer. Unfortunately, we'd sold all the beer at the market, so I didn't have any more to sell.

Chinon is famous in our region for its red wine. I don't know how well known the wine is in the rest of France though, and in England it was not well known at all until very recently. It's an incredible wine. Lots of people don't like it at first. It's a difficult wine to get into. I often hear people describe it as 'earthy'. I don't think it tastes earthy. It can be thin, it can be acidic; it's a complex, light-red wine that smells of pencil shavings and is made from Cabernet Franc grapes. It's not obviously a nice wine, but the more you drink it, the more you get out of it. I'm not brilliant at describing wines – at a tasting at the *cave des vins* in the wonderfully named village of Panzoult, one of the best wine villages in the Chinon *appellation*, when asked to described the smell of a particular wine, I panicked at being put on the spot and went with 'candyfloss and concrete fly-over supports' – but I would say this: there are much easier wines to drink, like Côtes du Rhone, the round, easy-drinking southern wines, cheap Bordeaux. These wines are like the popular kid at school who goes on to become a used-car salesman. Chinon is the nerdy kid at school who becomes a multimillionaire rock star, marries a transvestite and invents cancer-free cigarettes.

I remember being taken around by an estate agent when we first came to the area and being amazed at the some of the houses we passed as we toured the countryside around Richelieu. Majestic buildings set back from the road behind imposing gates.

'There are so many châteaux around here,' I said.

'Those aren't châteaux,' said the estate agent, 'they are farmhouses. But there are lots of châteaux too. That, for instance, is a château.' She indicated to the right. A stone wall ran along the road for what must have been a kilo-metre, split by a set of imposing gates and a magnificent gatehouse. As we passed the gates I saw a brief glimpse of a huge château in tuffeau set back half a kilometre up a drive lined with immaculately pollarded trees. The châteaux, the grand farmhouses, even the basic, long, single-storey houses you see have a delicacy that marks them out from other regions.

This particular area of the Loire is famous for its châteaux. The more we explored the area, the more of these châteaux we discovered. There are the big ones, the ones that you will find advertised by the tourist board, normally with some kind of historic significance – the châteaux of Chenonceau, Blois, Amboise, châteaux that Joan of Arc visited, châteaux where various kings and queens resided, but then there are also lots and lots of great châteaux that you would never hear about. Everyday châteaux hidden away behind rows of pine trees, built by the local big cheese. There are two like this between us and Richelieu that you wouldn't know existed unless you took a wrong turn or two.

Then there are these grand farmhouses, which I had mistaken for châteaux. La Ruche, our house, was a miniature example of one of these. One of the expats I gardened for, Roy, who had an absolutely beautiful house with a fountain and a maze, told me that a lot of the grand farmhouses like his were built in the nineteenth century when the railways arrived and allowed the farmers direct access to Paris. Suddenly everyone was incredibly wealthy and so they started building grander and grander houses, trying to outdo each other. The chimneys on the houses were a status symbol; the bigger the chimneys the wealthier you were. Never could there be a better example of the manifestation of one's insecurities around the size of one's johnson.

You can pick up a genuine château for a little over €500,000 and a grand old farmhouse for less. Compare

La Ruche.

The family with some of their menagerie.

Gadget the miniature horse and Burt the satanic dog.

Rose, Albert and Tommy with that woodburner.

Chinon.

Early on market day in
Richelieu.

The
brewery
in the barn.

Enjoying a beer with Burt.

Tom's ancient van.

that to what that gets you in London – which illustrates the reason I needed to leave London, actually. We were slowly being squeezed to death. Services were being cut, rent was going up, the cost of living was getting higher and higher while our wages stalled. Some people were still getting disgustingly rich – expensive restaurants and designer shops continued to open and flourish, while the rest of us were gradually being fooled into thinking that living on the limit was OK.

Old houses were divided into as many flats as the developers could squeeze in. New flats were built with the minimum possible space that the regulations allowed – kitchens combined with living rooms combined with bathrooms, so you could cook your bacon in the morning while simultaneously watching Eamonn Holmes and taking a poo. Unfortunately not *on* Eamonn Holmes. And yet still no one could afford to buy these flats. They say people in London don't know their neighbours, but thanks to the build quality of the walls in my block, I knew more about my neighbours than they'd tell their therapist.

Local pubs were shutting down every day because of the cost of rents in the capital and short-sighted, money-grabbing breweries. The only way pubs could survive any more was if they were caked in widescreen TVs and so full that there wasn't a seat in sight and every journey to the bar was like hacking your way through a medieval battleground. Drinks were just on the limit of what you could afford, so that you couldn't get nearly as drunk as you wanted. Not a café without a queue outside the door in the entire city.

It was impossible to drive anywhere without being stuck in traffic, no matter what time of day or night you travelled and then, if you were lucky enough to find a parking space, it would cost you more than your battered old car was worth. Everything was monetised. Everything was designed for profit first and the minimum possible service next. Nothing was done with the primary intention to make us happy any more and we'd been fooled into thinking this was OK. Some kind of sleight of hand had taken place whereby money was no longer a means to an end – it was the end.

Here was different. Here, you needed enough to live and that was it. Once you had enough to live, just being in a nice place with nice food and nice wine was enough. The problem I had was that I couldn't even get us enough to live.

I was having a breakdown on a ride-on lawnmower over at Andrew and Sarah's house when Aunty Maggs rang. I don't mean the lawnmower had broken down, I mean I was crying uncontrollably while riding round and round in circles without even engaging the blades, listening to 'Fernando' by Abba on repeat while Burt smirked at me from under a bush. You see, I was wondering what the hell I was going to do. The market had been brilliant, but once the dust settled I realised I hadn't made any money from it; indeed, once everything had been taken into account, I had lost money. All it had done was shown me a tantalising glimpse of what might have been. I felt sure the demand for a microbrewery was there – I mean, 300 bottles sold in one and a half hours! That was extraordinary. But it had taken me a month to make 300 beers, so there was no way I could meet the demand or make any money while I was still brewing with the GrainFather. Now I was back mowing lawns and further away from affording a brewery than ever. It was heartbreaking.

'You still interested in some investment for your brewery?'

'Oh, what? Um. Hi, Aunty Maggs.'

'Well?'

'Well, I suppose so. I mean yes. Definitely.'

'Brilliant. I'll give you three grand. The only thing I ask is you name one of your beers after my dog.'

'OK, um, sure.' I couldn't believe it. I switched off the engine. 'Are you sure about this, Maggs?'

'Of course I'm sure. Just name a beer after my dog.'

'Right. No problem. What's your dog called?'

'Mussolini.'

'Mussolini? Like the—'

'Mussolini.'

'The guy that—'

'Mussolini.'

'Oh, right. I see.'

It was a crossroads moment. Just when all had seemed lost, I now had a chance to haul myself back from the precipice; my life wasn't over after all, but to save myself and my family I would have to dispense with any morality and name my beer after a fascist dictator. Would I stand by my morals and do the right thing, or would I sell out?

'Right. Of course. Mussolini . . . I'd be happy to.'

'I'm joking, you idiot. She's called Biscuit. You didn't really think I would call my dog Mussolini?'

'No, of course—'

'Don't tell me you were actually going to name your beer after a fascist dictator.'

'Well, I mean, technically I would be naming it after your dog, you see, and anyway, I believe there's still a market for that sort of thing in some areas of central Europe . . .'

'Look, never mind. Name a beer after Biscuit and consider it a deal. Send me your bank details and I'll transfer the money. You're very brave, you know, giving up your life and moving over there — what you've done and everything. We all think so.'

'Thanks, Aunty Maggs. I really don't know what to say. Has your house fallen off the cliff yet?'

'Not yet. I'll need that three grand back when it does, so you better get moving.'

She hung up. I was in a state of disbelief. Three grand could just about buy me the brewery I needed. Everything had switched around with one phone call. If there were clouds in the sky they would have parted.

I texted Rose: *The hawk is in the pantry. I repeat, the hawk is in the pantry.*

Rose's reply: *Have you been drinking again? I told you not to drink near spinning blades.*

I was puzzled for a moment until I realised I had only just made up the code for 'everything is going to be OK because Aunty Maggs has just invested three grand in the brewery'.

I texted back: *It's code for everything is going to be OK because Aunty Maggs has just invested three grand in the brewery! The hawk is in the fucking pantry!*

Well, you'd better bloody well buy a brewery quickly, before you piss it up the wall. Start looking! she replied. And so I finished my mowing, chased Burt back into the car and started looking.

I've never thought of myself as brave, so I was pleased Aunty Maggs thought I was, but after a while I began to think that maybe in my case 'brave' was the wrong word. There are two sorts of people who give up perfectly acceptable lives and risk it all on a completely new start. There are brave people who think it through, see all the risks, and do it anyway. Rose was brave. Then there are people who don't give it any thought at all. People who just assume it will work out fine. Those people are idiots. As far as I could see, it seemed to be working out fine.

BEER NO. 8:

Mussolini Ale

RECIPE	MISTAKES
4.2 kg Pale malt	Not adding crystal malt
500 g Munich malt	Not pushing Burt out
200 g Biscuit malt	of a moving vehicle
200 g Melanoidin malt	Failing to defend myself
25g Syrian Goldings hops at 60 minutes	against the Gallic shrug
20 g Saaz hops at 10 minutes	
25 g Huell Melon dry hops in the fermenter	
500g local honey	

Burt had rolled in fox shit. This became apparent several minutes into a three-hour drive to the Charente-Maritime region of France. I was running half an hour late, so turning back was out of the question. I believe Burt knew this. He was in an unusually upbeat mood.

I was on my way to look at a microbrewery that had been advertised for sale on leboncoin, a website that is the French version of eBay, although they also have eBay. The whole situation was typically French. I had been searching every website that had advertisements for second-hand breweries from the moment Maggs called. These were exciting times. Up until now each brewery I had enquired about had already been sold. This was the first one still available.

I resolved to push on despite the wretched stench emanating from Burt, slouched on the passenger seat next to me. I wound down all the windows I could reach and put the pedal to the floor of the 1999 Renault Mégane estate, which had almost zero effect.

The brewery was just outside of Angoulême in the Charente region, which runs along the west coast down to the Dordogne. It was a glorious day of sunshine. I had not visited Angoulême before, but it was a pretty region of steep, green hills like jelly moulds, similar to the Yorkshire Dales (I've never been, but I've watched *Last of the Summer Wine*), except these hills were striped with vineyards growing grapes for Cognac, and scattered with tumbledown farmhouses with terracotta roofs.

Three men in their sixties greeted me when I arrived in their little village. Bruno was the owner of the brewery. His two mates helped him out with it. It was a small brewery, capable of making about 300 litres of beer per brew, which was just what I was looking for. I presumed he'd show me round, but when he invited me into the kitchen it was clear there was no question of going to see the brewery straight away. First, we had to try the beers. This is how it is done in France. It is never purely just a transaction. It's an opportunity to talk, to drink and to eat. We've forgotten to do that in the UK and we are the worse for it. We drank Bruno's beers, a blonde beer, an amber beer and a brown beer. Whereas in the UK we classify our beers as bitters, milds, ales, IPAs, lagers, porters, stouts, imperial stouts and several other classifications that I've no doubt forgotten, the French have always traditionally defined beer by its colour. This is changing as the craft beer movement gradually makes its way across Europe, but it's still the norm in much of France.

It turned out Bruno's two mates were retired, and with them, Bruno, previously a fishmonger, had spent the previous ten years making beer and selling it at the markets in the seaside towns on the south-west coast. They'd had a fantastic adventure, but now he wanted to retire. I liked the three of them. They sat around the table taking the piss out of each other relentlessly.

Once we'd sampled all his beers, Bruno showed me the brewery. It was situated in a converted garage that had been tiled, and it was absolutely batshit. An ancient riveted metal water heater that looked like a deep-sea diver's helmet from *Twenty Thousand Leagues Under The Sea* and used to be part of a Cognac still was bricked into the corner. He'd converted a large rectangular metal trough that he used to keep eels in into the mash tun. Various other old bits of fishmongery paraphernalia had been recycled into brewery equipment. It was innovative, it was marvellous, but it was completely insane. He performed the sparge, the washing of the grains once they've soaked, with an old shower nozzle. I couldn't buy it. I wanted to, but I didn't have the courage. He made very good beer from it because he had built it and he understood all the quirks of it, but it was way too crazy for me, so I had to decline. I could see he was disappointed when I told him I couldn't buy it and you would think that would be the end of the transaction, but instead – and this was the measure of the man – he insisted I stay for lunch, so I did. It was an hour of good food and outrageous slurs directed at everyone they knew.

For the next two weeks, searching for breweries for sale became an obsession. Several times I was close, but even when I phoned up a few minutes after a listing for a brewery had appeared online, I still seemed to miss out.

After two weeks an advert for a brewery that was just what I was looking for came up. I phoned up immediately and, unbelievably, it was still available.

'I'll take it!' I said before the man on the other end of the line had even finished his sentence.

'Don't you want to see it?' said the very reasonable man, called Antoni.

'Maybe. Where is it?'

'It's in North Wales.'

'It's where? What the hell is it doing there? It's supposed to be in France.'

'It was on the advert. It's where I live,' said Antoni, slightly taken aback. In my frenzy to find a brewery, I had forgotten that I had widened my internet search to the UK as well as France.

'Oh. OK. No, just send it over. It will be fine. Do you think it will be fine? It will be fine.'

'Well, it's not the sort of thing you can send by post. These are four-hundred-litre vats we are talking about.'

'Right. Got you. OK, I'll phone a delivery company. I know one that delivers to this part of France regularly.'

Within minutes of the phone call I sent a bank transfer through for the deposit, despite not having done any research on the brewery or finding out how much it would cost to be delivered. You see, with a big life decision such as this, I always say it's best not to think about things too much, because you'll probably talk yourself out of it. I have lived my life by that philosophy and on the whole it's delivered below-par results. But I find it's best not to think about this too much.

The brewery arrived three weeks later. I knew of a delivery man called Stephen who ran a removals firm based in the north-west of England that specialised in taking things to France and back. I had met him when I was gardening over at the Johnsons' and he had turned up to remove some of their stuff. Stephen's motto was: 'My nan always said I could do anything I wanted. She just didn't tell me how.' I knew he'd be the man to bring the brewery to France. He reminded me of a character from a Douglas Adams novel.

Antoni had impressed upon me the importance of getting a removals firm with a truck with a tail lift, as the equipment was extremely heavy, but whenever I told Stephen this he told me not to worry, he didn't have such a truck, but he wouldn't need it anyway – his nan had told him he could do anything, etc. And lo and behold, on a lovely May morning his truck arrived all the way from Wales and reversed through our gates in Braslou, taking with it several branches of the overhanging laurel. I later found out from Antoni that the only reason they had managed to load the brewery equipment at their end was because some lads from the factory next door had seen them struggling and had lent them a forklift truck. It was therefore unsurprising that Stephen appeared to have no idea how he was going to unload it at my house.

Eventually, after several cups of tea, Stephen and his mate decided to set up two long, thin metal ramps close together, the sort of ramps you use to get cars onto trailers, and roll the equipment off the lorry and down the ramps on a pallet truck, which Antoni had kindly donated along with the brewery equipment, with me and his mate in front stopping the pallet truck from moving too quickly. For the first two vats – the mash tun and the boiler – this was fine, but the last vat – the hot-water heater – weighed half a tonne. As Stephen tipped the pallet truck onto the ramp, it immediately picked up momentum. Courageously, we all let go and dived for cover. It shot down the ramp on the pallet truck and smashed through the gate to the back field, eventually coming to a stop next to a startled Cameroon lamb (did I tell you a Cameroon lamb had arrived? I assumed it was something to do with Rose's pregnancy cravings, which was odd because Albert was almost a year old). There was a pause while the giant vat teetered on the pallet it was sitting on before coming to a stop, mercifully still upright.

'OK, that seems to be everything,' said Stephen, satisfied with another job well done. 'Good luck with the brewery. We'll pop by for a pint next time we're down.' And off he went on his next absurd adventure.

Using the pallet truck, Rose and I shifted the vats across the garden into the little outbuilding that sits maybe thirty metres from our house as a miniature horse, a sheep, a Cameroon lamb, two chickens and two dogs watched curiously.

It actually made more sense for the brewery to be in the barn attached to the back of the house, rather than the outbuilding over the other side of the garden. There was already running water and electricity in the barn and there was loads of space, and that was where I had been brewing with my little GrainFather brewery, but I am nothing if not an all-round selfless guy.

'No, Rose. You should take the barn at the back for your art studio. With its space, high roof and bare stone walls it will make an ideal place to house your artworks. I'll set the new brewery up in the outbuilding,' I had said when we were deciding where the big brewery would go. 'And besides, if I am all the way over the other side of the garden, it will be much easier for me to drink morning beers without being told off,' I didn't add. But that was basically the driving force behind the move. And so it was decided. My new brewery would be over in the outbuilding on the far side of the garden, away from the house.

It was currently full of old gardening equipment, logs and woodworm. Incidentally, I have never seen a woodworm, and I don't know anybody who has. Make of that what you want. The outbuilding was built out of irregular blocks of white stone; it had two rooms on the ground floor, of which I would take one, and a hayloft that was only reachable by ladder.

I set about tearing out all the crap that was in there. The further back I got into the room the older the stuff was, until finally I was pulling out huge wooden rollers, cogs made of iron and other bits of machinery, which, I realised eventually, were parts of an old wine press. It felt like an archaeological dig. I was pulling out genuine relics from a time gone by. I chucked everything in the dump.

Next, I needed to get electricity and water into the outbuilding. I had no idea how to do this, but luckily Damien once again came to the rescue. He explained we would need to dig a trench about a metre deep from the house to the barn and lay the pipes and cables from the house to the outbuilding in the trench. Damien's friend Pascal, the local builder and one of my most loyal black-market customers, lent us a mini-digger on the proviso that I gave him lots more beer. Damien's other friend, Bastien, would connect the mains water pipes for us. Damien dug the trenches with Pascal's digger a week or so after the brewery had arrived. Everything was on track. After that, we had to plumb the brewery in. I asked Damien if he knew a good plumber and − I'll never forget this moment − he turned to me and said: 'Yes, I know a good plumber − you.'

'What do you mean, Damien?'

'You are capable of this, Tommy. You can do it. I believe in you.'

I was almost moved to tears. Damien actually thought I was capable of doing something practical. Warm with pride, I waited till Damien had left and then I phoned Hervé the plumber.

Once Hervé had done all the plumbing, things were progressing very well. I thought I'd probably have the brewery up and running by the end of May, maybe mid-June at the latest. All I needed to do was get a more powerful electricity supply to run the brewery. I assumed a simple phone call to EDF, the electricity company, would suffice.

Three months passed.

'You didn't validate the *rendez-vous*. That's the problem. That's why the engineer didn't turn up,' said the man from EDF. It was now August. The brewery had been ready but for the electricity for almost three months.

'But you didn't tell me to validate the *rendez-vous*. How do you validate the *rendez-vous*?'

'You have to phone us up.'

'But I phoned you up last week and the week before and you said it was all OK.'

'That was before I knew you hadn't validated the *rendez-vous.*'

'You didn't what the what? Now, listen to me. You've been messing me around for months. Please, please send someone over. I just need you to increase our electricity. I have a family to feed.'

'Absolutely. Once you go back and make a fresh application online. We should respond within six weeks.'

'I can't wait another six weeks!'

Although we were on the phone, I knew that his reply to this would be a Gallic shrug. Gallic shrugs are one of a French person's most powerful weapons. I remember my first telling encounter with a Gallic shrug was a month or so before. We'd had a problem with the 1999 Renault Mégane estate. The battery had stopped recharging. I bought a new battery, but it still wouldn't recharge. I replaced the alternator but it still wouldn't recharge. I took it to the garage.

'The problem is your new battery. It's faulty,' said the man at the garage. 'You need to take it back to the shop.'

I took it back to the shop. They tested the battery.

'The battery is fine,' said the man in the shop. 'It's probably your alternator.'

'But the alternator is new and the man at the garage told me the battery was faulty,' I said.

Now here's the interesting thing. If it was the UK, the man at the shop would have done one of two things – he would either have accepted responsibility and swapped the battery, or he would have blamed the garage owner for making a faulty diagnosis. My guy, however, simply shrugged. A Gallic shrug! And that was it, end of conversation. Before I knew it, I was back in the car with the battery on the passenger seat next to me, in a queer state of perplexedness. I drove back to the garage.

'Did you get a new battery?' asked the man at the garage.

'No. They tested the battery and they said it was OK,' I said.

Now, here's the other interesting thing. In the UK, the man at the garage would have said one of two things, either:

'Your man at the shop is in the wrong.'

Or:

'OK, we'll have another look. Perhaps there's something else going on.'

However, my man said neither of these things. He simply shrugged. A GALLIC FUCKING SHRUG! And that was it. And as far as I can see there's no counter to it. The way they do it, and it's very clever, means that's automatically the end of the conversation. It's so powerful that you just sort of walk off, and by the time you realise nothing has been resolved, you're half a mile away. And so, sandwiched between Gallic shrugs, the car went into semi-retirement. The only way to get it going was to manually charge it the morning before you wanted to drive it. A crazy situation, but, thanks to the Gallic shrugs, no other options existed.

Now here I was on the phone to EDF, once again banjaxed by a Gallic shrug. I was at my wit's end. I hung up.

'Mama,' I whimpered, slumped on the living room floor. 'MAMA!' My mother, thankfully for her, was several hundred miles away in England. But that gave me an idea. My mother wasn't here to make everything better, but there was somebody similar who perhaps could. Madame Leclerc! The Mayor of Braslou!

Ever since we'd moved in, Madame Leclerc had been extremely supportive. Yes, there was a period where she had started trying to avoid me, but this was my fault. We had been told by several expats that the thing to do when you move to a new village is to go and introduce yourself to the mayor, so when we first rented the house in Braslou we went and introduced ourselves. Back then we spoke really bad French and the conversation ran as smoothly as a sledge ride through a speed-bump factory, but she was still very friendly and pleased that we'd made the effort. But then, a few months later when we returned to the village to actually buy the house, I thought to myself, *Well, we've bought the house now; that means I should probably go and see the mayor again.* Rose refused to come this time. She couldn't understand why we would need to introduce ourselves again, but it was clear to me that our status had changed, therefore another meeting was required.

It turned out Madame Leclerc couldn't work out why I had come to introduce myself again, and soon after I sat down in her office, I couldn't understand why I had either. There was nothing to say that hadn't already been said, so we sat there in silence for several excruciating minutes. Finally, she managed to persuade me to leave. For a few months after that if she saw me coming she would duck into the nearest doorway, terrified no doubt that I would try and introduce myself to her again. She must have thought I had suffered a brain injury that had destroyed my short-term memory. But that was all in the past. Now I had something very real to talk to her about.

When I walked into the office, for a brief moment Madame Leclerc thought about hiding under her desk, but once I explained my problems with the electricity company she was enraged on my behalf. Nobody fucks with a citizen of Braslou when Madame Leclerc is in charge. She phoned

EDF immediately. From the look on her face it seemed they started giving her the same spiel that they gave me. And this is where it turned wonderful.

'OK, I am going to stop you there. I am the Mayor of Braslou,' she said firmly. Not aggressively, because she didn't need to be aggressive. The hardest man in the pub isn't the one that walks around shouting at people and tearing off his shirt. Everyone knows who the hardest man in the pub is because he as an aura. The mayor has that aura. I could tell that the temperature in the office of the guy on the other end of the phone suddenly dropped by a couple of degrees.

'That's better,' said the mayor as the phone conversation continued much more to her satisfaction. I could only hear her side of it, but it was clear she was now on top.

'Yes, he doesn't speak very good French.' She winked at me.

'Yes, perhaps he is a bit simple.' She winked at me again.

'OK, thank you for your cooperation.' She put the phone down. 'They'll be over on Monday,' she said.

I don't suppose there are speed-bump factories, thinking about it.

Over those three months, the EDF months as they will be known in history books, I gardened badly, I spent time with my baby son, who incidentally turned out to be a right laugh, and I brewed with my GrainFather.

We held Albert's first birthday party shaded from the heat of the June sun by the walnut trees in the dingly dell between the house and the brewery, our friends and neighbours gathered either side of two long tables covered in red-and-white chequered tablecloths, a wheelbarrow full of ice and bottles of Fred's fizz, and an absolutely extraordinary spread of cakes and scones assembled by the combined force of our two mums, the likes of which could summon type 2 diabetes from the clouds. After the party, Monsieur Richard, David Kimber Bates, Michael the English builder, my father and I, directed both spiritually and physically by Damien's dad, Claude, dismounted the heavy brewery equipment from the pallets and set it in place.

Throughout July and August, we spent glorious days canoeing down the Vienne from Ile Bouchard to Chinon with Ali and David, willows overhanging the river concealing sandbanks and beaches perfect for picnics, stopping off to swim in the river, which is wide enough to divide countries and yet shallow enough that you could wade from one side to the other, gently burning the upper dome of one's beer belly in the endless run of sunshine.

We had dinner parties in Mishi's converted barn in amongst oil paintings and dozens of old kitchen dressers that Mishi had bought and painted and subsequently forgotten what she was going to do with them.

We knew enough people that someone always needed unskilled labour. Apart from the gardening, I did other bits of work wherever I could find them. Mostly lifting things, cutting things or smashing things.

I focused on the brewery and did all sorts of work I never thought I would do – fixing up insulation, knocking holes in walls, constructing evaporation pipes, pointing stone walls and various other tasks that are actually fairly straightforward.

Nick showed me how to do the pointing. Nick is obsessed with pointing. He's repointed miles and miles of walls round his house in Faye-la-Vineuse. I worry that one day he'll run out of things to repoint and he'll start repointing things that shouldn't be repointed, like air vents and plugholes and the entrances to mineshafts. I could sort of understand the addiction. It's a bit like messy play. You mix up your pointing concoction of sand and lime with a bit of water in a wheelbarrow, and then you splat it all over the walls with your hands, filling in all the holes. Then, after an hour or so, once it's started to dry, you brush off the excess pointing concoction with a wire brush and slowly the stones beneath it are revealed in all their glory, like relics in an archaeological dig. Having said that, I tired of it after a day or so, so one wall of the brewery looked brilliant and the rest looked like turd. But what can you do?

Perhaps my most surprising achievement during the EDF months was the construction of a wall. We'd had to knock down part of a three-foot-high stone wall that runs through the front garden when we dug the trench from the house to the outbuilding so, with a little instruction from Damien, I attempted to rebuild it myself. The results were extraordinary. I managed to rebuild it to such a poor standard that it if you stared at it for long enough it actually looked like it was tumbling down before your eyes, and yet it remained standing. It was a sort of Magic Eye picture. Many a passing Frenchman found this hilarious and, added to the worst fence in Braslou, I realised I was starting to turn the house into a theme park for bad DIY. If the brewery didn't take off, I could start charging an entry fee to local tradesmen to wonder at my crap building projects.

My beer, however, was improving all the time. I developed the 'Biscuit' beer that I'd promised my Aunty Maggs I would. It was based on the Belgian-style amber ale I had been making. I added Biscuit malt, a Belgian speciality malt that adds a bready taste to the beer, making it fuller, and I found if I dry hopped it with a little bit of a hop called Huell Melon, it gave it an extra dimension.

I gave beers to Damien to try, I gave beers to Pascal, I gave beers to anyone I could. Generally, people liked the beers. My IPA was still too bitter, apparently, even though it wasn't, and Damien and Monsieur Richard kept telling me I should make a blonde beer, but apart from that the feedback was good. I changed the grain bill – the quantities of malt – for my porter beer so that it was less bitter and more chocolatey. I was desperate to get out and start making beer to sell, but the EDF months were proving to be a financial catastrophe. Once again, our money was being stretched to the limit. My nan's alarm clock returned.

'Darling, now really, you must listen to this. I've bought a traditional flat-bottomed Loire river boat from a guy near Chinon who smokes the most extraordinary amount of dope.' It was Mishi on the phone.

'Oh, right. I see. You've bought a boat?'

'Yes, a boat. That's not why I'm phoning, of course.'

'No. Right. What can I do for you.'

'I'm phoning because I've also bought a tower.'

'You've bought a tower?'

'Yes, sweetie, a twelfth-century tower in Chinon. Would you be a sweetie and move some furniture up to the top? I'll pay you, of course. And there'll be bacon sandwiches.'

'OK. No probs, Mishi.'

Mishi had indeed bought a tower. I spent a day lumping antique furniture to the fourth floor and back down to the bottom as Mishi changed her mind several times a minute in between making bacon sandwiches and chai, this incredibly strong, sweet tea that she'd discovered when she lived in India.

She seemed so exhausted with deciding where the furniture should be that there were moments where I thought she was going to cancel the whole thing and sell the tower there and then to a passer-by, but eventually she settled on where she wanted everything. I always liked working for Mishi because she was interesting. She would talk on all manner of subjects at the same time – fine art, parking regulations, she would tell me about when she worked with the Beatles in the '60s, and she made incredible bacon sandwiches.

With this and the other odd jobs I'd done over the summer I'd gathered together a little bit of cash, but the EDF months had killed me financially. I'd given up some of my gardening jobs in April expecting instead to be brewing through the summer. My aunt's money had disappeared into the brewery and then, with perfect timing, the 1999 Renault Mégane estate decided it had had enough. The garage couldn't fix the problem of the battery charging, but they did manage to identify a separate, terminal problem with the gearbox. It wasn't the ideal vehicle for me anyway. Now I needed something bigger to take to market. Something that could take tables, fridges and lots of stock.

Actually, I should tell you how we ended up buying the 1999 Renault Mégane estate in the first place. It was when we were staying in the village of Chantelle in the Auvergne region of France, back when we first came over and we were child-free, carefree and flush with a rapidly dwindling redundancy pile. This was before we came back to Braslou to buy the house.

We needed a new car for three reasons:

1. Driving a left-hand-drive car in France was safer than driving a right-hand-drive car.
2. Rose had a ceramics exhibition down in Provence and we needed more space to transport her pieces.
3. I had just crashed our other car into a ditch and written it off while trying to find my favourite radio station – Radio Nostalgie.

We had a week to find a new car before our contract at our house there was up and we had to drive five hours over to a campsite near Bordeaux. I remember walking past a car at the village garage that was the most awful-looking thing I had ever seen. It was a Renault Mégane made in the 1990s – the decade that brought us two-tone jeans and the Lightning Seeds. God, I hate everything about that decade. You can say what you like about the '80s, but at least they had passion and ambition. The '90s barely even went through the motions. It started off terribly with grunge music. *Grunge music.* That turd on a string. Listening to grunge music was like finding a shit in your butter dish. You spent the rest of the day wondering why anyone would do something so inexplicably horrid. But at least they didn't wash. After that they sanitised everything and the rest of the decade beiged out into the horizon. It wasn't that the music was dreadful, or the style was dreadful, it was that it wasn't really anything. It was the Lightning Seeds. One day some-one will steal the 1990s and nobody will fucking notice.

To say the Renault Mégane was badly designed gives it too much credit. It wasn't designed. Nobody dared design anything in the 1990s. It was an off-white void on wheels. It had nothing to say for itself. It was the physical embodiment of the noise you make when you chew salad. Worst of all, it was an estate version. I remember thinking to myself at the time 'at least we won't end up with that shit-cube'.

I wanted to buy a classic French car – a 1970s Citroën shaped like a streamlined lemon – but it rapidly became obvious we didn't have anywhere near enough money. Instead we turned our attention to modern, practical cars, but they were too expensive as well. Most used-car dealerships in France only sell cars that are one or two years old, so the prices were still quite high.

Now we were running out of time. I trawled through every single used-car dealership for thirty kilometres and found nothing. Our tenancy was up in two days.

I switched my search to the internet and soon found something we could afford a few miles away. It was called a Fiat Doblò. It was a sort of utility vehicle crossed with a people carrier and It was the first in Fiat's new range of cars designed by a drunken toddler looking through a kaleidoscope. It was remarkable in that no elements of the car matched any other elements. No windows were the same size or the same shape, none of its parts were the same proportion. The bonnet looked further away than the rest of the car. If you stared at it too long it gave you an attack of vertigo. Needless to say, I quite liked it.

Sadly, before we could buy it, someone else saw the genius in it and bought it. And so it got to the day before we were due to get thrown out of our house and still we had no car. Luckily there was one car left in the village that nobody in their right mind would ever buy. The 1999 Renault Mégane estate.

I resented that car for a long time, but despite its age and

161

its general nothingness, it dragged us around France and gradually I developed a grudging respect for it. But now it was on its last legs it was time to move on. It was time to do the decent thing and leave it in the garden to get overgrown with weeds until Rose bullied me into one day getting it scrapped. It was time to look for a van. The problem was, I didn't have the money to buy one. We were in a bind. Rose's father happened to be staying with us.

'Well, perhaps I could invest a little in the brewery, if you really need it,' he said when he heard my predicament.

It's embarrassing borrowing money from people. You should be proud and strong and dignified. You should insist that you don't need it. No, it was a kind offer, but it was time for me to stand on my own two feet.

'You're a great man. How does five grand sound? I'll dedicate a beer to you,' I said immediately.

'Fantastic. Perhaps we could name a beer after my grandfather?'

I thought for a moment. 'Was he a fascist dictator?'

'What? My grandfather?'

'Actually, never mind,' I said. It wasn't a deal-breaker either way.

The new beer was named Clifton Porter. And with that, the search for a van began. Something modern, safe and reliable. Something I could depend on.

'Does it have air con?' I asked.

'No,' said the seller.

'Sat nav?'

He laughed. 'No, it does not.'

'Is it economical with fuel?'

'Not really, no.'

'Reliable?'

'It's thirty-five years old, so no.'

'Heated seats?'

'No.'

'But it's pretty safe though, right?'

'It doesn't have seat belts.'

'Oh. Hey, does the siren still work?'

'Yep.'

'I'll take it.'

'OK.'

'Actually wait, let me ask my uncle. Tony, you think I should buy it?'

'God no,' said my uncle Tony.

'OK ... I'll take it.'

Tony sighed and started walking back to the car.

'Oh, yes,' said the seller, 'I forgot to mention, you can't lock the doors.'

Tony stopped for a moment. Surely no idiot would buy a van that you couldn't lock?

'Why not?' I said.

'Because it doesn't have any locks on the doors,' said the seller.

'Oh, right,' I said.

Tony shook his head urgently and made a swiping gesture across his throat.

'I'll take it,' I said.

Tony sighed and started walking again.

I was never one of those children who was really into fire engines, so it was as much of a surprise to me as it was to everyone else that I decided to buy one. Fire engine is perhaps an overstatement. It was a little red *pompier* (fireman's) Peugeot J9 van made in 1982, a hilarious design with both the front and back wheels situated so close to the middle of the vehicle that it rocked back and forth on them like a toy boat. It was round and irresistibly cute, but when you drove it you soon found that within a monster lurked. A monster that cared little for adequate brakes and a halfway-sensible turning circle. Tony was right to try to persuade me not to buy it. The damned thing was a wreck. Not only that, there are certain alarm bells that should ring when the person you are buying it from:

Refuses to tell you his address.

Insists on meeting you on a roundabout on the outskirts of town and transporting you to a secret location where the fire engine is stored.

Opens up on the defensive, telling you in a fairly aggressive manner that there is nothing to worry about, over and over again, then proceeds to argue away several problems the van may or may not have that you hadn't even been aware of, so that he sounds very much like he's having an argument with the voice of conscience in his head.

Ruins any attempts you had made to view him as an honest man by advising you that the best way to replace the faulty windscreen would be to smash it yourself and claim it back on the insurance, just like he did with that car over there and that other car over there.

In fact, all of these alarm bells did ring, but none of them rang as loudly as the genuine, working siren. There comes a time when you have to stop fucking around and make things happen. This probably wasn't that time, but nevertheless I went ahead and bought it. And besides, despite his air of shiftiness, I liked the guy selling it. He looked like Robert De Niro would if he'd made some bad life choices.

He clearly knew he was ripping me off. When I studied

the CT report – essentially its MOT – he broke into a cold sweat and started pacing the room. He was human, you see. He wasn't some kind of cold-blooded psychopath; he knew he was probably doing something shifty and he clearly wasn't at ease with himself. But I had a feeling he wouldn't sell me something that was dangerous: he wasn't that sort of guy. Maybe he had doubts about its reliability. Maybe he had stumbled across the van for free and couldn't believe how much I was willing to pay, so he felt guilty about that, but any van from the early 1980s is going to be unreliable. I was prepared for that. I had searched for a while for a van like this and this one was much cheaper than anything else on the market. It was none of my business what his profit margin was; the only thing that mattered to me was whether I thought the van was worth what he was asking, and I thought it was. It had a siren, for God's sake.

Tony wasn't the only one to try and dissuade me from buying it. When I had shown Damien the advert, he had told me not to buy it. Celia had told me not to buy it. Rose had definitely told me not to buy it. They all thought I should buy a modern, practical van with power steering, but they couldn't see what I could see. Underneath all that rust was a beautiful, 35-year-old Peugeot J9 fireman's van in some semblance of working order. A giant ladybird on wheels. A design classic. And let me ask you this: if you are in a busy market surrounded by all manner of delicious food and drink, what is going to grab your attention more: a white Ford Transit with side airbags and a decent service history, or a 35-year-old fire engine with flashing lights and a fucking siren? Maybe the brakes worked, maybe they didn't, but it had flashing lights on the roof and a siren. I forgot to mention it had flashing lights. It had flashing lights.

The problem I had now, having bought the fire engine, was that I had to get it from Burgundy back to the Indre-et-Loire. I'd found the van on the website leboncoin, and the bloody thing was in Burgundy, you see. Burgundy is hundreds of miles from Braslou. The whole thing was ridiculous. It was idiocy, I tell you, and yet, unsurprisingly, this is what I did. My uncle Tony happens to live in Beaune in Burgundy, quite close to where the van was, so that's why he'd come to see it with me.

Having bought the van, we drove it back to Tony's house, a terrifying twenty-minute drive full of near misses and failures to stop. There I stayed the night, debating whether to try and drive it all the way back to the Indre-et-Loire the next day or to spend a few hundred pounds getting it towed home. Tony told me not to try and drive it home. Damien and Celia told me not to try and drive it home. Rose definitely told me not to drive it home. Even Bad-Life-Choices De Niro, a man who had gone to great lengths to fib about how reliable it was, had told me not to drive it home. Except for the odd test drive to the end of the road and back, the van hadn't moved for twenty years or more. Braslou was four-and-a-half hours away by motorway, and I couldn't take the van on the motorway anyway because according to Bad-Life-Choices De Niro it wouldn't really do more than 70 kph. A quick check of Google Maps revealed I could cut across country and avoid the motorways and it would take six hours.

I decided to drive it home. I knew in my heart it would make it.

The next morning, I set off at 7 a.m. and picked my way through the villages and vineyards that surround the Burgundian town of Beaune. I soon regretted my decision

166

to try and drive it home. I was convinced I could hear noises from the engine that weren't there the night before when we drove it back to Tony's. A noise like a bass guitar from somewhere above my head grew louder and louder while at the same time a sound like a sea lion being whipped by an angry dinner lady gradually began to develop from the engine, and yet it continued to trundle along.

After two tense hours, I was in the Morvan – a vast and remote national park to the south-east of Burgundy. Most importantly, it was a hilly park. The van was still forging ahead, but it disliked going up hills immensely, often slowing almost to a halt as traffic built up behind me. I realised that on the downward hills I would have to pick up as much speed as I could in order to carry that speed up the next hill. And so, as I mounted the crest of each hill I would slam the van into fourth gear (it only had four gears) and push the accelerator flat to the floor. Gradually the van would pick up speed and the engine, which had been unusually and imaginatively placed in the actual driver's cab just to my right, where one might normally have a middle passenger seat, would begin vibrating and groaning, so that I could hear every piece of it rattling and spinning, and as I approached the bottom of the hill and stared at the rising road in front of me, the speedometer creeping up to an ill-advised eighty kilometres an hour, we would begin to climb. For the first few yards the van would hold its speed and I would scream with delight. But then the engine would start to strain and, sure enough, the speed would drop, slowly at first, but as momentum disappeared it would crawl slower and slower and cars would pile up behind me, the drivers gesturing and pulling out menacingly, even though it would be suicide to try and overtake on these roads. I would rock backwards and forwards, trying to will the thing over the top, all the time waiting for one of the ancient, decrepit engine parts to crumble into dust, which would at first stop the van in its tracks and then see me roll backwards down the hill into anything behind me, as the handbrake, Bad-Life-Choices De Niro had told me in a rare moment of honesty, was working at just under 25 per cent capacity. And yet the engine parts didn't crumble and still the van trundled forward, scraping its way to the top of hill after hill, until finally we rolled out of the Morvan and onto more sympathetic roads.

I was perplexed as to why the designer of the Peugeot J9 had decided to put the engine in the passenger seat, but I soon realised the big advantage of this was you needed only to reach over and touch the plastic engine cover to discover whether and to what degree the engine was overheating. At first it seemed to get to a near-terminal heat every two hours or so, at which point I would pull over for a few minutes to let it cool down, but as the sun rose and began to sear the tarmac in front of us, stops became more frequent until I was stopping every half an hour.

As I passed through towns and villages, locals sitting outside cafés pointed, children smiled and waved. I met them all with the steely grimace of a fireman who had saved a thousand lives and was on his way to save a thousand more but didn't consider himself a hero, although he clearly was.

I stopped for lunch at 1 p.m., six hours after I had set off. By my original calculations based on Google Maps, I should have been almost home, but I was actually only just over halfway. Seventy kilometres an hour is really fucking slow. The town was called Dun-sur-something-or-other, or Something-or-other-sur-Dun, as I recall. A nice enough place. Glassy-eyed locals chatted to me about the van as they drank Pernod on the terrace of the local bar, which faced onto a square surrounded by lime trees. I was directed to a restaurant near the church and ordered their *menu du jour*, which was appalling. I'm still haunted by that leg of duck confit that slithered round the plate in figures of eight in its own slime.

As I walked back to the car, I was followed by an angry teenager blasting aggressive rap music very loudly on his phone. At first, I wondered what he had to rebel against in this perfectly nice town. Then I realised it was probably the food.

'Duck confit.' I nodded and rolled my eyes in solidarity as I got in the van. Then I attempted what I hoped might be a gang sign for Something-or-other-sur-Dun – I made my thumb and forefinger into a loop and poked my other finger through it. He was confused. There was no time to explain. I had fires to put out.

On I chugged through the increasingly benign countryside and endless fields of sunflowers, through the department of Nièvre and on into the department of Cher. *This must be where they built the never-ending pop-singer robot, Cher*, I thought to myself. Despite its uninspiring landscape, I was impressed, and serenaded several farmers with Cher's 'Believe' as I passed them by. There's a chance I was suffering from mild heatstroke. Now it was early afternoon and the temperature in the shade was up to the mid-thirties. The engine beside me was red hot and it was almost impossible to cool it down even when I pulled over because it was so hot outside, so on I went, plundering the bars and cafés of central France of any booze they had to offer while I waited for the engine to explode. But it didn't explode, and finally the houses in the villages I rattled through began to turn to tuffeau stone and I knew I was getting close to home. Twelve hours after I had set off, I pulled into Braslou.

'What the hell is that?' said Rose.

I shouted out of the window, over the noise of the spluttering engine, 'THIS, MY DEAR, IS THE BEAST OF BURGUNDY. OR THE MONSTER OF THE MORVAN. I HAVEN'T DECIDED ON THE NAME. THE POINT IS, THIS IS GOING TO MAKE US A FORTUNE.' Rose didn't seem convinced. 'IT HAS A SIREN,' I added.

Several days later I took the van over to my friend Dale's to see about getting it fixed up. He lives in Saint-Gervais-les-Trois-Clochers about twenty minutes away, so forty minutes away in the van, and he paints cars for a living. Dale eyed the van up.

'OK, we've got two options. Either we can give it a quick coat of paint in your garden using rollers and just cover all the rusty bits, or I can restore it properly in my studio. What will it be?' asked Dale.

'Properly restored, of course. The J9 is a classic. A piece of French history. When you take ownership of a van such as this you owe it to the nation of France to restore it. You are obligated to do everything in your power to make it great again, as if you'd found a masterpiece faded and torn at the back of your barn. It's a work of art. You'd restore a work of art, wouldn't you?'

'OK. Well a complete restoration, including knocking out all the dents, fixing the rusted parts and professional painting, and you're looking at three thousand euros.' Dale looked at me for a moment. 'You just want us to roller over the rust, don't you?'

'Yep.'

BEER NO. 9:
Clifton Porter

RECIPE	MISTAKES
4.2 kg Pale malt	Not adding Crystal malt
1 kg rolled barley	Failing to defend myself
500 g Chocolate malt	against the Gallic shrug
200 g Roasted barley	
25 g Nugget hops at 60 minutes	
50 g Mandarina Bavaria dry hops in fermenter	

The town of Saumur, which stretches along the banks of the Loire about half an hour west of Chinon, is like Chinon's older brother – they look quite similar, but whereas Chinon is still innocent, Saumur has a stash of pornos under its bed. I should say these are outrageous slurs I'm about to make about Saumur and I have absolutely no proof of any of them. But it's what I think.

Like Chinon, Saumur is a picturesque medieval town built in tuffeau sandstone. It is famous for its military riding school. It's bigger and grander than Chinon. Like Chinon, it has a fortress/château looming above it. Unlike Chinon, it has an opera house, which for my money makes it a den of sin. Any town with an opera house is smutty. No one goes to the opera to listen to opera. This is my thinking. They go to opera to visit brothels afterwards. That can be the only reason you'd sit through four hours of constricted howls in Italian. That must be what opera is all about. That's why people still do it. Opera is a front for smut and the pages of porn magazines washed up under hedges.

I recommend visiting Saumur. Not for the brothels that I imagine exist, although when one enters a smutty town there is a base thrill that is undeniable, but because it has winemakers and restaurants and the École Nationale d'Équitation – the famous military riding school that puts on performances of horses doing what they are told every week. We went to see a particular performance of horses doing what they were told once for Rose's birthday, and although it was remarkably dull, they did play opera music, so it was obviously a front for smuttiness. Most of the show was incredibly stuffy in a way only the military can really pull off, but they had one act – an act called 'family rock' – that was memorable. It was clearly the manifestation of what some elderly general thought would appeal to young people. The act consisted of a man, two women and two children, all in Lycra outfits designed, I'm fairly sure, by one of the local brothel madams, performing acrobatic tricks on horses to the sound of bad music. I presume the name was ironic, as they were the least 'rock' family I have witnessed. They performed the cheesiest routine ever devised. What I found most interesting, though, was that there were two women and only one man. It must be assumed, because they were French, that one of the women was playing the role of mistress and this added a real frisson to the display.

The wine towns in the region – Chinon, Saumur, Bourgueil – have the money, but there are other nice towns around us. Châtellerault, where they used to have a hand-grenade factory, and Loudun, a medieval town that still has some of its ramparts. These other towns are often referred to by locals as 'run down'; they're towns you wouldn't have heard of unless you lived in the area, but compared to their equivalents in England, such as Stevenage or Basingstoke, they are splendid. These are historic towns: they have towers and castles and medieval bridges and an old hand-grenade factory.

Richelieu, for me, is the most interesting of all the towns in the region. It's unique: a walled, moated, seventeenth-century 'new town' founded by Cardinal Richelieu and designed by the architect who built parts of the Sorbonne and the Louvre, Jacques Lemercier. I've never heard of the guy. It's built on a grid with two great squares, one at each end of the town. One square is said to represent the monarchy and the other the Church. They are connected by the Grande Rue, which is lined on both sides by the most elegant four-storey townhouses, with great courtyards hidden within each of them. There is a cathedral-like twin-spired church and turreted gates on all sides of the town, all dating from the seventeenth century and still to this day almost completely intact. It has a magnificent park on the southern end. A park so magnificent that the gardens of Versailles were based on it. It should be famous throughout the world. It was called 'the most beautiful village in the universe' by the French poet Jean de La Fontaine. I've never heard of the guy.

But there is a reason for its lack of fame. There is a tragedy in Richelieu that dates back to the nineteenth century, and you can still feel it in the squares and the symmetrical roads. You can see it on the faces of the Richelais – the people from Richelieu and the surrounding area. The cardinal didn't only build this incredible town, you see, he also built a château in the park. I'm not talking about a large country house – I'm talking about a vast complex of buildings that ran from one end of the park to the other. The most enormous, extravagant castle, all designed by Jacques Lemercier. A château with the biggest collection of fine art in Europe. A château that was the envy of France.

The cardinal died and the chateau was passed to his family. But a century and a half later, during the French Revolution, his family were banished. When they returned they were destitute and had to sell the château. By now it was in a state of disrepair. And here is the tragedy. It was bought by an *estate agent*. Disaster. Any normal person would have realised the significance of the place, thought about the long-term effects of having such a château attached to the town, and set about restoring it, but this fucking estate agent, some kind of nineteenth-century equivalent of a polyester-suit-wearing, girlfriend-cheating, mobile-phone-stuck-up-his-arse, branded-Mini-driving, bloody estate agent drenched in Lynx Fucktard, this small-minded shitty-knickers of a man decided to dismantle the château and sell it off brick by brick for a quick profit, thus tearing the heart out of the place. So there is a feeling of vertigo in Richelieu. A confusion. A lack of confidence. It's still a town that should be famous – it has enough about it without the château – but there is a sense of something that could have been much more. The Place du Marché should be lined with hundreds of cafés and restaurants like the harbour in Honfleur on the Normandy coast. Instead there are a couple of cafés and the rest of the buildings are garages, offices or old hotels that have been derelict for years.

They haven't given up, though. It feels to me like Richelieu could be great again. It's just been connected to Chinon by a *voie vert* – a cycle path along an old railway line that should mean more tourists coming in. They are growing in confidence. Since we've lived round here a couple more restaurants have opened up. They are planning classical concerts in the park in summer. If it still had the château though, what a town it would be.

'BURT DESIST!'

It was too late. While I'd been centering myself on the loo, Burt had somehow managed to unlock the gate to the back paddock and was merrily chewing on the neck of one of our chickens. I could swear he winked at me as I walked round the corner to see this scene of horror. I chased him half-heartedly round the paddock, but I knew it wasn't going to achieve anything, so I went back to the house and phoned Rose. Rose was in Cornwall staying with her mum.

'Burt has eaten one of our chickens,' I grassed. This was serious. Rose liked those chickens. I thought this might be just enough of a crime to get him sent away to a home for dogs with criminal minds. I could feel Burt glaring at me from the garden.

'Oh no,' said Rose. She was genuinely upset. This was good. Things were going perfectly. But then she said, 'Although I suppose when you think about it, he only did what we do every week. Except he didn't get his from the supermarket. In fact, his was free range. Much better for the environment. If anything, we're the ones at fault,'

'But he ate one of our chickens!' I said.

'Better that than a battery chicken.'

How Burt had come out of this as the good guy I didn't know, but I was boiling over with impotent rage.

Later that day I shoved Burt into the van and the imaginary arguments began again. I'd started having imaginary arguments with Burt just after Albert was born. A side effect of the caffeine, perhaps. Sometimes he had a gruff Yorkshire accent. Sometimes he had a gruff French accent. No matter how much I tried, he always won the argument. He would finish with, 'Told you, you rubber duck prick.' On this particular occasion, while I started off on the offensive, it transpired that Burt was furious with me for grassing on him about the chicken and he gave me a verbal beating that left me cowering in my seat.

We were making the journey back to the malt house in Issoudun. In the new brewery I used ten times the amount of malt per brew as I did with the GrainFather, so trips to the malt house were going to be frequent.

The van rumbled along to Issoudun quite happily. It took nearly twice as long as it would have in a car, and the van rattled so much that by the time we got there the wing mirrors were pointing in completely the wrong direction, but it got there. Whereas last time when I arrived in the Renault Scénic they brought the malt out packaged up on a wooden pallet only to be told of my plan to strap each individual bag of malt into the seats like a family of dumpy children, this time they looked with wonder upon the freshly painted Beast of Burgundy as they loaded the entire pallet into its ample *derrière*. Yes, they laughed as well. They laughed at it not having power steering, they laughed at the smoke pouring out of it and they laughed at the fact it was still rocking back and forth several minutes after rolling over a speed bump, but I felt that in general they had gained a new-found respect for me and we would one day be able to embrace each other as men.

Burt's chicken farts started on the way home. Something about eating an animal with a still beating heart hadn't agreed with him and he became extremely unwell. The odour was abominable. Whenever he farted he looked up at me to gauge my reaction. He enjoyed watching me clutch my throat.

We were pulled over by a routine police check a few miles out of Issoudun.

'Everything OK?' said the young gendarme.

No, it was not OK. A murder was taking place. A murder by chicken fart. The first of its kind. I looked at Burt. His severe admonishment for being a grass was still ringing in my ears.

'Yes, fine. All fine here,' I said. I gave him my details. As he checked my insurance documents, I mouthed 'help me'. The policeman looked confused.

'He's trying to kill me,' I mouthed silently. 'With chicken farts,' I added. Burt flashed me a glance.

'Are you sure you're all right?' asked the policeman.

Burt rested his head on my lap and stared up at me innocently.

'Yep, all good.'

'OK, on your way.'

'Tell Rose I love her.'

'What?' said the gendarme.

Burt growled.

'Have a nice day!' I said, and off we rolled.

It took all my will to live to survive that journey home. At times the smell was so bad I was close to passing out, but I visualised my son and that got me through. It represented a worrying new phase in my relationship with my dog. I'd long suspected he was plotting my demise. Now he was actively trying to kill me.

The van looked really, genuinely fantastic, thanks to Dale's expertise, even though we'd painted it using rollers in the garden. It looked better than I could have imagined. Dale is an interesting guy. Lots of people told us about him when we first arrived and no one had a bad word to say about him. Indeed, it seemed he had helped almost everyone out at some point. What they all, to a person, did say though, was that at first glance he might seem a bit scary. I think he's in his fifties. He's a muscular biker (the Muscular Bikers – possible band name) with long hair, a bandana and a pink goatee. He has a thick Brummie accent and he has no fear of saying whatever is on his mind. So you can see he would be absolutely terrifying to the meek middle classes.

Once you meet him, though, you realise he's a diamond. Painting the van with him was a pleasure. My personal highlight was Dale cutting his hand wide open on a piece of rusty metal and, rather than going to A & E, simply supergluing it back together and carrying on. According to Dale that's what superglue was originally intended for. It was invented in the Vietnam War. I haven't fact-checked this yet, but I suspect it's probably not true.

Dale loves it over here. He got sick of the UK just like we did and moved over here to be with his partner, Tamsin. He's the sort of person who has advice for any situation, all of it somewhat singular. When we first got our dogs he advised us, in order to get them to stay by our side, we should take them to the forest, let them off the lead and run as fast as we could. His theory was the dogs would be so scared at being left alone, they would chase after us and from that moment they wouldn't want to leave our sides. I tried this. As soon as I let them off their leads and ran, the dogs, astounded at their good fortune, turned and disappeared into the undergrowth, splitting off in different directions. I waited hours for them to return.

Dale has also recommended at various times pinning one's dog down and growling in its face to establish yourself as pack leader, holding your child's hand close to a flame to get them to understand the fear of fire and having a boxing match with teenagers who don't show respect at the dinner table. He's very much from the old school.

I chose an army-grey paint for the van. Firstly, it was a cheap colour to buy. Dale explained to me that there are certain paints that are used by the public services in France and these are much cheaper than other paints, presumably because they are mass produced. Secondly, it was the colour of a plastic German soldier I had as a child. From my recollection the soldier seemed like quite a serious, reflective guy but with a fun side when he'd had a few schnapps, until finally he got a bit handsy and he was put in a cab. That's basically a summary of my brand values. I got large transfers of the Braslou Bière logo printed in gold by a local print firm and stuck them to the sides.

I was really proud of my van. The failing brakes, the great plumes of black smoke it emitted as and when it felt necessary; it felt like an extension of me. So it didn't matter that I was a complete amateur at manoeuvring the thing.

*

The three vats stand against the bare stone wall at the back of the brewery as you walk in. Open pipework and electricity cables run round the walls. Pipes and wires are everywhere, attached to old stone and crumbling flaps of concrete. It's a beamed ceiling and between each beam are strips of layered silver-foil insulation. The floor is concrete, painted in several coats of garage paint that are already peeling and flaking. The water for the brewery enters through the heat exchanger, passing along the back wall to the first vat – the water heater. The water heater can hold up to 600 litres. This is because it takes 600 litres of water to make 400 litres of beer. You leave some water in the malt; you lose some water from evaporation.

From the water heater, the water passes into the mash tun – the middle vat. It's smaller than the other two. You add the ground malt to the mash tun and then you add the water from the water heater. It depends on the beer, but I tend to mash (soak the malt) at 65–69°C. As a general rule, the higher the temperature you mash at, the richer the flavour, but the less alcohol you get.

Soaking the malt like this converts the starches in the malt into sugar. After an hour or so, you drain the sugary liquid you've created, which is now called the wort (often pronounced *wurt*) through a false bottom in the mash tun, leaving the spent malt behind. The wort is pumped into the last and biggest of the three vats, the copper. The copper serves several purposes. Here you boil the wort for an hour or more to sterilise it. All sorts of complicated chemical reactions that I don't understand occur at this point. This is also where you flavour your beer with hops and other adjuncts like honey, fruit pulps, anything you like really.

Once you've finished the boil, you pump the sterilised

wort into one of the old plastic fermenters that stand along the left side of the room via the heat exchanger, which cools the liquid and refills the water heater with warm water. On the right hand wall are two old fridge freezers that store my hops and yeast. I have a couple of little tables on wheels that carry my labelling machine and bottling machine. To the left and right of the door as you walk in there are flimsy shelving units holding all manner of junk. Siphons, pumps, bottle caps. The brewery is dark and damp, lit by one tiny window and a couple of inadequate strip lights. I really fucking love my brewery.

'OK, switch the water on,' I said. This was the day I had been waiting for. The brewery was finally ready. I was about to do my first big brew.

'Are you sure?' asked my dad. 'Have you checked the connections?'

'For the thousandth time, yes, Father.' This was the relationship I had with my father. He was never convinced I was doing things properly. Well, maybe all those other times in my entire life he was right, but not this time. I was thirty-nine years old. I had a son of my own now. I was a man.

'Switch the pump on, Father.' I said in a deep voice.

The two of us stood in the brewery, staring each other down. This was the *moment*. In every father and son relationship there's a point when the balance of power shifts. When the son finally becomes a man and the father has to cede to him. The son becomes the head of the family because he is the stronger. The *moment*.

Dad switched on the water. Immediately an unsecured hose burst from its connection and flailed like a strand of Medusa's hair, spraying water – which I had carefully heated to 76°C – all over the brewery. I ran for cover behind a big plastic fermenter. My father didn't run. I can still see it now, the image of my father in the centre of the brewery as scalding rain poured down his face like tears of disappointment and *I told you so*.

We dried ourselves off.

'OK. Switch on pump two,' I said.

'Are you su—'

'Yes, I'm sure. Switch on the damned pump,' I said. This was definitely the *moment*. In every father-son relationship . . . Pop! A pipe exploded off its mounting and doused an electric heater in water, causing the whole brewery to short out.

'Oh, for fuck's sake, Tommy.'

Predictably, everything went wrong that first day. There was liquid everywhere: hot wort, cleaning products, blood. A saturated carpet of hops, yeast and wet malt had woven itself across the concrete floor. Whenever I plugged one leak, another, more powerful leak sprung elsewhere. Once the wort reached boiling point, the steam-extraction pipe that I'd run around the walls of the brewery, my finest feat of engineering to date, began dripping at every join of the pipe, giving the effect of being in some cave deep underground, because rather than sealing the pipe properly at each joint, I'd simply sellotaped it. *It will probably be all right*, I had thought. I know. Clearly, I hadn't completely learnt the lesson of Monsieur Richard. But with my father's help we eventually managed to pump the wort into the fermenter and pitch the yeast. I didn't have that father-son moment where I became the head of the family that day. If anything, that moment became further away, but we did make beer. If I'd had my way I'd have boarded up the brewery door and started over with a new brewery in a new location, such was the state of the place by the time we finished. It seemed to me impossible to clean it all up, but with the gentle cajoling of my father, we did clean it up.

The brewery was in good shape overall. The only issue was the fermenters. The brewery came with large, plastic 400-litre fermenters that were old and scratched. Antoni had told me that was his only concern about the brewery when I bought it. He suggested I should get new ones, but I decided to persist with the old scratched ones because I didn't want to spend any more money. At that point I didn't have any more money.

If you remember, I had had problems with plastic fermenters in the past. Repeating the same mistakes is a speciality of mine. I knew there was a chance that the fermenters wouldn't be completely clean because of the scratches, and there was therefore a chance that the beer would get spoilt in the fermenter. *It will probably be all right*, I thought. When I die in some brewery-related catastrophe of my own making, that will be my epitaph.

One of the most interesting things about refuse is it has a universal smell. That may be the only interesting thing about refuse. Obviously, there'll be different smells depending on what's in the refuse, but alongside those smells there's a general smell of refuse that is the same the world over. Normally I find it a reassuring smell, something stable to anchor you in an ever-changing world, but when I detected that smell in my first batch of beer from the new brewery I felt so low. The beer had fermented out fully and it smelt a little bit of bin.

It was those bloody fermenters. I knew I shouldn't have

used them. I had made the same fucking mistake again with plastic fermenters. It was insanity. I mean, it actually was insanity, repeating the same thing again and expecting different results. That's insanity, isn't it? I felt like such a plum.

This was the beer I'd made with my dad. My signature Braslou Bière, the red IPA with German hops. It actually smelt only very faintly of bin, but there was definitely a smell of bin.

That wasn't the only problem. It was also way too bitter. I'd made a mistake when adding the flavouring hops at the end of the boil. I had tried to cool the wort down below 78°C because below that temperature the hops no longer add bitterness, just flavour, but my thermometer had given me a false reading. When you have a large amount of liquid – 200 litres in my case – then you have to make sure you stir it well before you take a temperature reading, as some parts of the water can cool down much more than other parts. This is what happened, so when I added the hops it was actually much too hot and the hotter the wort when you add the hops, the more bitterness is extracted. In this case, much too much.

At this time, I was still testing the beer from the fermenter – I hadn't bottled it, so not all was lost. Sometimes when you bottle beer and it re-ferments in the bottle, it improves because all sorts of new chemical reactions take place (stop laughing at the back), so I decided to bottle it anyway and see how it turned out in a couple of weeks.

Champigny-sur-Veude is a village in between Richelieu and Chinon that has a hairdresser's, a couple of bars and, oh yes, a mind-blowing sixteenth-century chapel built in tuffeau with twin-domed towers. There are so many villages like it round here. Everyday villages with these spectacular historical buildings, monasteries, châteaux, etc. sitting in the middle of them and everyone driving past them as if they are a Sainsbury's Local. But the best thing about Champigny-sur-Veude is that it has wild hops growing along the banks of the River Veude. Madame Maciet alerted me to them.

The thing with my beer was that although it was made in Braslou, most of the ingredients weren't local, as some fat, bald, drunk prick took great delight in telling me at the Braslou *marché de l'asperge* back in April. This had annoyed me a great deal because he was mostly right. The malt was from France in general, but not necessarily my region of France, the yeast was from Germany and the hops were from all over the place – Alsace, Germany and in some cases America. What I should have said to him – and indeed what I do often say to him in my infantile imaginary recreations of the event,where I emerge triumphant and ride off doing a wheelie on a Harley-Davidson – was that 95 per cent of beer is made up of water and the water is definitely from Braslou.

Hops from the local area, though, that was a start. The thing with wild hops is you have no idea really what they are going to bring to the beer. You don't know how bitter they are or what sort of flavour they are going to give. But that's OK. That's part of the fun of it.

Hops are normally ready to harvest around October. You can tell they are ready because they feel dry to the touch and when you squeeze them a little of this yellow resinous ooze comes out. I went to the river in Champigny with baby Albert in the pushchair one Wednesday in October when I was on childcare duties. It made a nice change from the usual McDonald's and illegal cockfights. I'd been once or twice before, but the hops were still moist; this time the hops were dry and ready to pick. By the time Albert was crying with boredom, I had amassed a carrier-bag full. Probably enough to make twenty litres of beer in the GrainFather.

I made a straightforward pale ale, low on maltiness, clean, to let the hops come through. I chucked it in a fermenter and hoped for the best.

A couple of days later I was drinking a morning rosé with Nathalie, the woman who owns the property to the left of our house. Nathalie is extraordinary. She's done so much work on her house. She works on it with any time off she has: weekends, evenings, bank holidays. She does all sorts of jobs. Nathalie is a strong woman who rarely smiles, at least when she's talking to me, and she often seems perplexed when I remark on how incredible it is that she's almost single-handedly transformed the house. She's typical of the people round here. They have no idea how utterly remarkable they seem to sofa dwellers like me. It's an old *longère* building – a long building on one level with hay storage above that would have housed the farm workers and possibly some animals. Nathalie was in the process of converting it into a well-appointed four-bedroomed house that she intended to rent out. She'd just given me the guided tour. She'd done a very professional job. The real selling point of the house though, parked in the middle room, was a great bread oven built of bricks, which must have been the size of Mini Cooper, would have provided bread for the local area and was still in working order.

Despite this interesting feature, before long I had skilfully turned the conversation to me by banging on about me. I told Nathalie about the Champigny beer.

'You know there's a farmers' market in Chaveignes

coming up. A local beer would sell really well there,' Nathalie said. 'Pierre helps organise it. Hold on, here he comes now.' Pierre was Nathalie's husband.

A large red tractor rattled into the courtyard. I remembered for a moment back in London when people arriving on tractors would have been a big thing. Pierre was atop it, wearing nothing but an old pair of dungaree overalls. Pierre is a middle-aged guy, slightly balding, with round features, deep, warm eyes and a beard, and he often wears overalls unzipped to his navel and nothing else. He speaks with a country accent that even Damien says he finds difficult to understand, and he has all sorts of intriguing gestures. One of his favourites is a wiggle of the nose like the woman in *Bewitched*, often combined with a sort of pulling away of his head while he stares at you. I think it means somebody isn't telling the truth or something along those lines, but I don't really have a clue. He pats me on the shoulder and calls me *jeune homme*. He has a way with you that makes you feel good about yourself. Pierre is a great man and if he wants to only wear overalls unzipped to the navel, who the fuck are you to stop him? What have you ever done?

As it turned out, Pierre was delighted to see me. Over another glass or two of morning rosé he explained, with the help of Nathalie, who translated his French into French, that he was part of the *comité des fêtes* that organises the *marché fermier de Chaveignes*, an annual farmers' market at the village of Chaveignes on the outskirts of Richelieu. He had mentioned to the Mayor of Chaveignes that there was a brewery in Braslou and the Mayor of Chaveignes was very keen on me having a stand there. He wanted more local producers involved.

Now, the farmers' market in Chaveignes is big news. It

has a footfall of 8,000 people. I did some maths in my head that involved a lot of rubbing out of imaginary numbers scrawled in the writing of an eight-year-old who'd spent too much time watching YouTube and eventually I came to the realisation that I could sell a lot of beer there. If it went well I could make enough money to buy new fermenters. Not only that, it would announce my arrival to the wider area in plenty of time for Christmas. In truth, it had come about six months too early. I had my IPA that smelt a little bit of bin – there was no way I could sell that – and any other brews I did would have to be in the old fermenters, and there was a great deal of risk involved in that. *It will probably be all right*, I thought. The market wasn't till the end of the month so I could brew at least once more. So then and there I asked Pierre to sign me up for a stand. We drank more rosé to celebrate.

'Watch out. What is that? A bee? Shall we kill it?' said Rose. She'd just got back from another weekend in England and she was curious to see how I was getting on in the brewery. I was getting on just fine, thank you very much, Rose.

'Yes, Rose, that is a bee and bees are our friends. Without bees the planet wouldn't be able to pollinate itself. Basically, they help the planet have sex with itself. They are God's planet-sex lubricant. Or something equally as important. So next time you think about killing bees, picture a children's nursery burning to the ground because of global warming and think again.'

'It looks suspicious to me. They don't normally behave like that. It's like it's waiting for something. Are you sure you don't want me to kill it?'

'Look, Rose, I haven't got time for this. I'm creating a

beer masterpiece. My new, improved Biscuit Ale. This bee is tired and lonely. It's the end of the summer. It should be in its hive doing whatever it is bees do, but it's out here trying to make friends and I respect that. And besides, if you kill one bee, all the other bees sting you to death. This bee is my friend,' I said, as I poured honey into the wort that was boiling away and tried to stroke the bee.

'OK.' Rose shrugged and wandered back to the house.

Twenty minutes later.

'Jesus Christ, Rose! They're fanatics! They're like miniature suicide bombers. Bloody Isis with wings!' I whispered.

'I told you I should have killed it,' she hissed.

We were in the kitchen now, with all the doors and windows shut. We probably didn't need to whisper. Bees pinged against the window. The bee in the brewery wasn't my friend at all. He was an absolute shithead. He'd told all his stupid, furry little bee friends that I was making a great vat of sugary liquid and before I knew it I had been invaded.

At first it was just a couple of other bees.

'Aha, more friends! I'll call you Dinkle and Donkle. Or Faggsie and Banana guy.'

But then millions of bees burst in, too many to name, flowing through the door in one long dark ribbon, buzzing around and threatening me in my own home. I read once that instinctively we are more scared of spiders than other bugs because, historically, spiders have been the most dangerous bugs for humans. Well, scientists, time to change your science list written on graph paper – I tell you now that there is nothing more terrifying than the sound of a swarm of bees. There's something about this noise, the same emotionless hum emanating from more and more points dotted around you in the air that induces a fundamental terror. Before I knew it, I had fled the brewery, ducking through the door as they poured in above me.

'Why are you screaming?' asked Rose, poking her head out of the kitchen across the garden.

'I'm not screaming, it's a battle cry developed by human beings over millions of centuries when they have been invaded by bees,' I shouted as I ran.

'It sounds like you are screaming like a child. Is it supposed to sound like that? You'd better come into the house. They look like they are following you,' she said calmly.

'It's actually only men who are most comfortable with their masculinity who can scream like that, Rose. It takes supreme confidence and a hell of a lot of testosterone,' I whispered breathlessly, as Rose urgently shut the kitchen door behind me.

'Did you finish your brew?'

'Oh, bollocks. No. I had just pitched the yeast, but I was still pumping the wort into the fermenter. I can't leave the pumps on. I can't leave the fermenter open. Jesus, Rose . . . I'm going to have to go back in.' I gave a Rose the same look Bruce Willis gave when he decided to crash into that meteor.

'OK. Do you want shepherd's pie for dinner?'

'Yes, please . . . If I make it back.' I said, giving Rose the same look, but with a raised eyebrow.

'OK. Can you feed the dogs when you're out there?'

'Yes, sure. IF I'M STILL ALIVE,' I said.

Rose started doing the washing up. I put on my thickest coat, a parka jacket, put the hood up and zipped the coat up to my nose and marched out towards the brewery across the garden. It was a horror scene out there. Bees buzzed all around the garden. As I approached the brewery door a deep hum from within grew louder and louder. I counted to three and ran in. I ducked and bobbed. It was dark from the swarm. Bees dived at me, bouncing off the coat only to return for a second pass. I ran to the control panel in the corner and turned off the pumps. I hadn't managed to get all the wort into the fermenter, but most of it was there. It would do. I put the lid on the fermenter as quickly as I could, shut down the brewery and I was out. It must have only been a few seconds, but those seconds played out in super slow motion. Most importantly, the beer was saved and I was a hero. It was my second brew using the big brewery and I was making Biscuit ale for the market in Chaveignes. I needed this beer.

I re-entered the kitchen.

'Is that really a battle cry?' said Rose. 'It's just it really, really sounds like a child's scream.'

Sometimes I just go and stand close to my brewery. Big steel vats clad in strips of wood. By general brewery standards it is a small, basic brewery – no bells and whistles, a static mash, a control panel from a 1960s sci-fi film – but it feels strong, permanent and plucky, and when I am around it I am relaxed. I didn't like the scratched-up plastic fermenters so much.

It was mid-October now, two weeks before the market. I had to try my Biscuit Ale. I prayed for it to come out well. I poured a glass from the tap of the fermenter. It was a murky brown. It smelt unmistakably of bin. I knew straight away, that as much as I loathed the idea, I had to ditch this beer. Two hundred litres of beer is a lot to throw away. You could bathe in two hundred litres of beer. I contemplated that thought for some time. But I had no choice. It was much worse than the red IPA. This beer had a real depth of bin. It was completely undrinkable. It's a hard business making shit beer. You wait for weeks; the waiting is a killer. One has to be patient when it comes to making beer. I can't tell you how irritating I find this. And then you taste it, knowing that so much rides on it coming out well, and instead you find you've somehow managed to mimic the exact taste of refuse and you feel crushed.

It's interesting, if you Google 'off flavours in beer' you find great long lists of off flavours and the reasons why they taste like they do – bacteria, oxygen etc., but I couldn't find a single list that contained the off flavour 'bin', so at least I was forging my own path.

The only modicum of good news was the little plastic bucket of Champigny ale I'd made in the GrainFather came out pretty well, considering using wild hops is total guess-work. Normally you buy hops dried or even compressed into pellet form. These wild hops were still fresh, which meant they had much more moisture in them, so if you normally added thirty grams of dry hops, you couldn't add thirty grams of fresh hops and assume the results would be the same, because in real terms you'd be adding much less. After doing a lot of reading and a lot of scientific equations, I got drunk and tipped the whole bag in while listening to Bruce Springsteen. *It will probably be all right,* I thought. The results were an easy-drinking pale ale with a subtle hint of hops, quite green and earthy. It wasn't much of a beer really, but it was perfectly drinkable.

Interesting fact: baguettes are that long thin shape because originally they were used as a weapon to put in the spokes of invading cyclists.

You can't replicate French bread from a good French bakery. Even French supermarkets can't replicate French bread from a good French bakery. In the UK, now even more than ever, with the rise of the artisan bakery we make lots of great breads – rye breads, sourdough breads, other even more pretentious breads, but I have never bought a baguette in the UK that comes close to a bread from any of our three local bakeries in Richelieu. A good baguette has a crisp exterior that isn't burnt, is moist and elastic inside while still being light and can send an invading cyclist tumbling into brambles without significantly ruining its taste or form. British attempts are either hard and cardboardy or they are heavy like a cucumber.

If you go to the bakery in Chaveignes at precisely 9.15 a.m., they are taking the *pains traditions* – large rustic loaves of bread – out of the oven. Grab the loaf, give them whatever they want for it and get back in the car and drive like never before, drive like you've lived in France all your life. Sprint from the car to the kitchen. Cut the bread with whatever you have, an axe, a sword, it doesn't matter, and plaster it with Brittany butter stuck with salt crystals – little saline hand grenades that explode on your tongue, the bread still warm from the boulanger's oven. The butter will melt into its soft white flesh. Holy shit, even thinking about it now makes me salivate. It is an experience that cannot be surpassed. I can't remember why I was telling you this. It had something to do with Brexit, I think.

The fact that we called it Brexit says it all. That we needed such a crass, reductive, clickbait name just to get anyone to look away from their mobile phones long enough to give a cocking fuck tells you everything you need to know about the state we've got ourselves in. I can't see

193

myself moving back to the UK at the moment. There are a few things I will miss, though.

Bacon. It's a cliché I know, but every time I eat a piece of bacon, for a brief moment I love the world and everything in it. Especially big fat pigs. You can buy wafer-thin streaky bacon rashers in French supermarkets, but all it's good for is insulating around windows.

Takeaways. Round here you can get pizza and that's about all. If you go a bit further, to the bigger towns like Chinon and Châtellerault, you can get the sort of Chinese and Indian takeaways that you found in the UK in the 1970s, except they're worse, because the French are absolutely certain they know best when it comes to food. Instead of celebrating the things that make these cuisines different from French cuisine, like chilli and spices, they have largely got rid of the things that make them different, so that every curry tastes like a bland stew and Chinese food is reduced to fried pieces of battered salt. I miss proper curries that make you shit fire and brimstone for a month and a half.

Pubs. Oh God, how I adore pubs. Proper ones, not the fun pubs made of blond wood where teenagers and psychopaths go to drink fluorescent drinks in a fluorescent environment and finger one another. No, proper old pubs with brass, mirrors and chandeliers. And drunkards who keep themselves to themselves. That's always the sign of a good pub. A drunkard who's so happy with his surroundings he doesn't need to insult your appearance and tell you about the time he was kidnapped by Nelson Mandela.

French cafés are magical in their own way. Sitting outside a French café on a hot day drinking a little glass of beer is fantastic, but I realised the thing with French cafés and bars: when compared to English pubs they are not specifically designed to get you pissed. That is the underlying philosophy of a pub. It might serve food, have karaoke, who knows, but it exists ultimately to get you pissed. Pubs are much more comfortable than French bars. The Scandinavians can shove *hygge* up their arses because British pubs have been doing comfort forever. When you think about it, there's nothing better than a comfortable place to drink yourself unconscious.

Apart from that, France is pretty good. The UK is now so insular. I detected it when I was growing up. The seeds were there in the '90s when you could sense that things were starting to go tits up. I mean, just look at grunge music.

People were becoming greedier, and while society can support a few parasites, if everyone becomes greedy then it all falls to shit. But no one wants to blame themselves, do they? It's much easier to blame the foreigners, especially when you're chivvied along by large parts of the press. And yet, let me tell you as someone who's had a lot of experience of the French – we're still fundamentally the same, not only as the French, but as large parts of Europe. We eat, we drink and we slag off the Germans.

The French don't hate the English. They think we're ridiculous, but they're quite fond of us. Most of the French people I talked to about the UK leaving the EU were just disappointed. They felt sad for us and they couldn't understand why we would do such a thing. But when you think about it, it makes perfect sense that we did it. It's a classically British thing to do. Essentially what we did is what Brits do in minutia every day. We let our frustrations build. We didn't do what the French or Italians would have done, and shout and scream at each other, go on strike for all of October till something changed or let off enough steam that we weren't so bothered any more, and equally we didn't have rational arguments about our problems like the northern Europeans would have done. No, because we are so repressed, we just let our frustrations build and build and merge and multiply without being able to find an outlet for them until finally we exploded, we lashed out irrationally and now we regret it. I do that all the time. When you think about it like that, Brexit is no surprise to the British at all, and it is completely baffling for the rest of Europe.

I can understand people's frustration with the European Union – it's bureaucratic and you might not share its ideology – but I can just about guarantee the source of your problems isn't Brussels. Being a member of the EU might make your life a little harder or a little easier, but it's not the real reason you've got a shit life – and I say this as someone who knows from experience – the source of your problems, the ones that really matter, is almost certainly you being a big, stupid tit.

And so, to the latest example of me being a big, stupid tit. I had around 150 bottles of beer in stock that I'd made with my GrainFather brewery: fifty bottles of the Champigny ale and around fifty bottles of both the Biscuit ale and the Braslou IPA that I had made as test batches. They were good beers. I was pleased with them. For the market in Chaveignes I had two options:

1. Go with the 150 hundred or so bottles that I was pleased with and be sold out before lunch, possibly to the ire of the organisers, who could have given my stand to a market seller with proper stock.
2. Give up my stand at the market.

Those were my two options. Inexplicably, I decided to go for option 3: Try and sell the 400 bottles of overly bitter IPA that smelt ever so faintly of bin. I'd bring the good beers as well, of course, but I knew I'd sell them fairly quickly and then I'd have to try and sell the bin beer. Chaveignes was an all-day affair.

There was a sort of desperate logic to this decision. Selling 150 beers wouldn't net me enough profit to buy some new fermenters. Selling 550 bottles would. And it was clear I did really need those fermenters. It was an all-or-nothing gambit. From the moment I decided to do it, it felt like I had set off down a slide at the end of which lurked a muddy puddle.

Chaveignes is an immaculately kept village carved in tuffeau just a kilometre or two from Richelieu. You head out of Richelieu to the chocolate-orange roundabout (so named by expats because it looks like a chocolate orange, if you really needed an explanation). To the right is Braslou. To the left is Chaveignes. You drive through a brood of chickens that roams the fields and roads just past the round-about. It's very flat, is Chaveignes. It has a town hall and a pretty old church and not much else. The farmers' market takes place on the fields behind the town hall.

I'd been up most of the night carrying out the confusing and depressing task of trying to label beers that I didn't really want to sell. I went to bed at 3 a.m. In the morning I met with Damien at 7 a.m. and we headed down to the market. I was exhausted before I had even arrived. Trying to get the van onto my pitch took nearly twenty minutes of shuffling backwards and forwards as Damien looked on in despair through clouds of oily smoke. Despite being almost exactly ten years older than him, my relationship with Damien was inverted – he took on the role of the older brother who'd been forced by his mum to take his embarrassing younger brother out to the park with all his mates. I would do stupid things and he would be tarred by association. I often felt he wished he could break free and leave me on my own, but he was too good a person for that. There was some moral obligation to look after me that he couldn't shake. The fact that I had a van full of beer probably helped as well.

After the *marché de l'asperge* in Braslou I had carved out a niche for shaming myself trying to drive vans at marketplaces, but this time it was particularly galling, as my audience were the men drinking wine at 8 a.m. at the booze tent opposite my stand – the men I admired most.

Once I was set up it was OK. The morning sun rose directly in front of us, reflecting off the gold lettering on the side of my van. I set the bar and table up in front of me with my Braslou Bière banner across it. I put my labelling machine on the end of the table to finish off the bottles I hadn't labelled and this proved to be a stroke of accidental genius because it gave an *artisanal* look to my stand and started drawing people over immediately. With the van in the backdrop, the stand looked fantastic. Incidentally, the quest to be *artisanal* is what it's all about at these places. Firstly, if you're seen as *artisanal*, it gives you an authenticity that means you can charge more for what you are selling and secondly it means you can get away with all manner of errors.

'The beer is flat.'

'That's because it's *artisanal*.'

'The beer isn't clear.'

'Well, of course it's not. It's supposed to be like that because it's *artisanal*.'

'The label on the bottle is upside down.'

'Um, durrr! That just shows it's *artisanal*, guys. C'mon.'

'Your clothes are covered in stains. Wait a minute – are your trousers on back to front?'

'Yes, because I'm being *artisanal*, you bloody prick-tits.'

Damien had the pitch next to me and had erected all his sculptures on plinths. He saw it as the perfect one-two punch. People would get drunk on my beer and then buy a sculpture that they would only realise they couldn't afford when they sobered up.

I put all my 150 or so good beers out. And they were good beers. The Biscuit beer especially was very nice. I thought briefly about just selling these beers and then going home, but I knew that would mean finishing up by mid-morning and trying to manoeuvre the van out of a packed market, and there was no way I'd be able to do that without innocent casualties. And the thing was, as I've said before, I *really* needed the money. I needed to sell as much beer as I could and besides, *The bin beer is all right*, I told myself for the thousandth time. I knew it wasn't, though. That was the stupid thing. One of so many stupid things.

It was an unusually hot sun for late October, and as the day progressed I began to sizzle and rouge (Sizzle and Rouge – good name for a *Eurovision* pop duo if it ever comes to that). Damien was very helpful at first, helping man my stall when he didn't have any clients, but around mid-morning catastrophe struck – he sold a sculpture for €500. He spent the rest of the day celebrating by alternating between pinching beers from my stand and drinking wine at the bar opposite. As he became more and more drunk, he punctuated his drinking routine with naps behind my van. And as he became even more drunk, he started sneaking into my van when I wasn't looking and switching the siren on, scaring the absolute shite out of anybody within a 200-metre radius.

My beer sold reasonably well in the morning. The hours of 9–11 a.m. aren't the most conducive for selling beer, but nonetheless I had a steady stream of customers. As midday approached there was a surge. Rather than smashing back the beers all day, people in the Richelais tend to drink one beer as an *apéro* before a meal – a sort of pre-food loosener. Just at the point where it became overwhelming, Damien's father, Claude, appeared beside me again like a guardian angel and started helping out on the stand, and his presence alone once again calmed everything and everyone. By the time it died down, I turned to thank Claude, but he had gone. Disappeared into thin air, or possibly the wine tent opposite.

The problem was that I was fast running out of the good beers. In my van, lurking like filthy little demons, were box upon box of second-rate beer just waiting to jump out and ruin my reputation. *It's not that bad*, I told myself. As my supply of good beers ran out, so I was forced to start putting the second-rate bin beer out. I tried a bottle. The aroma was good. First taste was good. *It's really not that bad!* I thought to myself. But then as I drank more, it began to get bitter. And there was the sort of a flavour of bin, just an ever-so-subtle hint of kitchen bin. It got more bitter. By the end it was definitely unpleasant. I finished my bottle. *It's not that bad*. So I started to sell it.

I think if it had been a truly horrible beer it would have been all right. Firstly, I wouldn't have sold it. Secondly, if

I had tried to sell it, people wouldn't have bought it. But this was sort of OK, but not really OK. It was mediocre. It started off OK, but by the time you were halfway through the bottle it was so bitter you may as well have been sucking lemons out of David Van Day's rectum. People tried it. They didn't really like it, but they bought it. Some didn't, but quite a lot did. Some people didn't even try it; instead they bought bottles because they wanted to support a local business. They bought it out of politeness, and they bought it because they trusted that I had made a good beer, and that killed me. The more it sold, the more a great spectre of regret loomed up behind me. Suddenly I didn't want to sell it any more, but it was too late. I'd put bottles out on the table. People wanted beer. When people asked to buy a box, I wanted to shout, 'No! Don't do it!' but instead I dutifully took their money and released another six bottles of substandard beer into the environment, off to float around kitchens and dinner parties, just waiting to pop open and ruin my reputation. Because that was what I had started to grasp, far, far too late. It was my reputation in each of those bottles.

I remember after the Braslou asparagus market in April, sitting in the hairdresser's as two pensioners talked about my beer, not realising I was the brewer.

'Is it any good?' asked old lady number one. There was an agonising pause.

'Not bad,' said the other old lady.

Not bad! I was ecstatic! I thought for some time about getting that tattooed on my neck.

But now, after the disaster in Chaveignes I saw it would work the other way round. There'd be endless conversations around the salons of Richelieu about how awful my beer was. Word would spread. That old granny from the hairdresser's would be furious.

By the time the market finished I had sold almost everything and I felt terrible. Physically I was broken and morally, for selling that beer to those poor people, I was a turd. That it had probably destroyed my reputation gave me some comfort. At least there would be justice.

'You liked the beer, didn't you?' I asked Damien.

'No,' said Damien.

'How come you drank so much of it, then?'

'If I can piss it, I drink it. Now let's go.'

Twenty minutes of shuffling the van backwards and forwards out of my pitch followed as the men at the bar shook their heads, before finally we trundled back to Braslou in convoy. I turned left into my house, Damien turned right into his. We didn't even say goodbye.

That night Rose called from England.

'How did the market go?'

'Yeah, it was pretty good, I suppose. I sold a lot of beer.'

'Why do you sound so sad?'

'Because most of it tasted of bin. I think I might have really messed up this time, Rose.'

'What do you mean *this time*? You always really mess up. Don't worry, Tommy. They'll forgive you. Anyway, we'll be back in a couple of days. I think Albert is missing you. He keeps pointing to a yoga ball and saying "Dada".'

A cat arrived. I assumed at first it was to do with Rose's pregnancy cravings, which was odd, as . . . well, you know. We called her Miss Marple because we were watching *Miss Marple* at the time and thinking up new names is exhausting.

The older you get, the more aware of winter you

become. The longer it feels and the more dread it inspires. It turns out this applies to the old 1982 Peugeot J9 *pompier* van as well. When I first got it, it would start first time without fail. Now, as the cold crept across the slate-tiled houses of the Richelais, the van became more and more temperamental, sometimes taking several minutes to get going. I felt very much the same.

I held my breath for most of November, wondering if my reputation had been ruined before I'd even really begun. Gradually I began receiving feedback about the beer from the market and generally it wasn't good. People did not like the beer that tasted of bin, which wasn't a great surprise, but interestingly it seemed that it wasn't just because it tasted of bin. It was too bitter. That wasn't a surprise either, really. I knew it was too bitter. What was a surprise was that people felt the good IPA I had made in the little GrainFather brewery was also too bitter. This was a beer I was quite proud of. The small amount of Biscuit ale I had had proved to be reasonably popular, as ever, but the most popular beer of all was the beer I made from wild hops in Champigny. To me, at least flavour-wise, it was the least interesting beer I had made. And then I finally realised what people had been trying to tell me pretty much from the beginning. Nobody round here wanted some super-hoppy, trendy, exotic IPA. They didn't want me to blow their minds, to shatter their world views; they just wanted a nice, easy-drinking beer made locally. Damien had been saying this all along. So had Monsieur Richard. I just hadn't listened. When I thought about it, almost every person locally had said they thought my IPA was too bitter. Some liked it, but it wasn't really what they were after. I had been so extraordinarily arrogant that I completely missed it. I thought I knew what people wanted to drink more than they did.

The most stupid thing of all was that I didn't have to stop making an IPA, I just had to make a blonde alongside it. The more I thought about it, the more I couldn't understand why I hadn't done that. So I set to work making a beer the locals wanted. A strong, blonde, Belgian-style beer. That's what Damien liked to drink. I would name it Berger blonde. Berger was Damien's surname. I texted Damien to tell him my plans.

'*D'accord*,' replied Damien. I had thought he might be a little more excited about getting a beer named after him, but after the last market he was probably worried it would turn out to be poisonous.

I used to think that using sugar in beer was a cheap way to boost the alcohol, but as I drank more and more Belgian beer, I realised that actually, in the good beers, this wasn't the case at all. Whereas if you use a lot of malt in your beers to get a lot of alcohol, the flavour from the malt becomes deafening to the point that after one or two bottles it can begin to get unpleasant. If you use less malt but instead add candied sugar to raise the alcohol, you get more subtle, palatable malt flavours but retain the rich, glutinous mouthfeel, a thick gloss over the malt, the upshot being you can drink loads of them without your tastebuds being scorched. This is because starch from malt is only 60-some thing percent convertible (stop laughing at the back) and so the other 40 per cent is giving you malt flavours, wheras sugar is 99 per cent convertable and adds no flavour but just increases the alcohol content. I think this is how Belgians make strong blonde beers that still taste quite light.

With my new Berger beer I decided to do this, except I

didn't have any candied sugar, so I used local honey to boost the alcohol. I think honey gives the beer a richer, viscous mouthfeel and local honey means local flavours. Apart from the honey, the recipe was a fairly straightforward blonde beer recipe: pilsner malt, a little bit of wheat and an Abbaye yeast, which gives flavours of banana and clove. For an IPA you want to use a fairly neutral yeast so that the flavour comes from the hops, but Belgian ales tend to draw much more of their flavour from the yeast. The only other slightly interesting thing I did was use Huell Melon hops for flavouring, rather than something more traditional like Saaz or Tradition hops, just to give it a little bit of fruit. There are a million blonde beers in France. You need to stand out somehow. I did a test in the GrainFather. It came out OK. A couple of tweaks and I would have something.

Some positives came from the market. Firstly, I did indeed make enough money to order some new fermenters. Secondly, with an all-day market like that you end up meeting hundreds, if not thousands of people, and almost everyone wants a chat. It melts your brain, particularly having to try and speak so much French, but it's great for contacts. I met several of the local bar owners there, as well as a restaurateur from Paris. I managed in the most part to stop these people from tasting my bin beer, instead inviting them to come to the brewery before Christmas to taste the new brews.

Jean Thomas, a guy I had met a couple of times at Braslou football club, asked me if I would like to have a stall at the truffle market just before Christmas in Marigny-Marmande, the village down the road from us, which he helped organise. It would have been a great market to do – Marigny–Marmande is the truffle capital of central France, so the market had a big footfall and the people who went had money because they wanted truffles and truffles were expensive. I told him I would think about it, but I couldn't bear the thought of another market at that point.

I was also approached by Agnès the saffron lady, so called because she sells saffron. She explained to me that she was putting together a cooperative of local producers to start a farm shop in Richelieu. It was launching at the end of November and they were really interested in stocking my beer. That was an absolute stroke of luck. Because it was a cooperative of sorts, I could sell beer there and take home much more of a profit that I would have if I'd sold into a private shop. This was a definite lifeline. It was crucial that I had some good beer for the shop. As much as I wanted to give up, I went back to the brewery. My new fermenters hadn't yet arrived, so I had no choice but to try another of the old plastic fermenters. I wasn't yet confident in my blonde beer and I decided not to try and force another IPA on the people of the Richelais, so instead I tried brewing a batch of my Belgian Biscuit ale.

One thing was clear: whatever happened, if I was to have any chance of rebuilding my reputation and starting to unpick the damage I'd done at Chaveignes, I had to make sure I put up an impeccable beer. Anything other than that would be marketing suicide.

Big, meaty, sweaty ballsacks. I'm not shitting you, this was what the beer I sold to the farm shop tasted like. After everything I had done at the market, I was now doing this. I had cleaned the last old plastic fermenter like never before, but, needless to say, it hadn't worked. The beer had fermented horribly. This wasn't the only problem. The elements in my copper, the tank you boil the beer in before you ferment it, weren't working properly, so I wasn't getting a strong rolling boil. If you don't boil your beer properly you can get high levels of dimethyl sulfide (DMS). DMS gives the flavour of corn. As well as this, if your sanitary practices aren't up to scratch you can develop diacetyl in the fermenter. This can give a buttery flavour. What they never mention, though, in any of the beer textbooks is – and this is the thing – they never mention that DMS combined with high levels of diacetyl give beer a taste like big, meaty, sweaty ballsacks. Once more I was breaking new ground in the brewing world.

It was a catastrophe of a beer. A real shit soup, and yet I still took this beer to the shop to sell. I drove the van full of shit soup down to Richelieu to deliver it to the shop one morning through stubbly, frost-covered fields thinking, *What the fuck am I doing?* But I couldn't stop myself. It was as if my body had become detached from my brain. I am prone to self-sabotage every now and then, normally when I am having some kind of crisis of self-esteem, but this was extreme.

Everything was out of control. After the market in Chaveignes I found I had around fifty or sixty bottles of the bin-flavoured IPA left. I hated these bottles. Every time I looked at them they reminded me of my failings and so I began to drink them. Night after night, as many as I could. There's a phrase they use in poker: 'on tilt'. It's where you have lost a lot of money on a big hand and instead of cutting your losses, you begin acting irrationally to try and win it back. You can no longer think logically and you start betting more and more and making worse decisions. I was on tilt.

And so it was that my opening beer at the shiny new shop designed to showcase the brilliance of the local producers tasted of sweaty ballsacks. I sold eighty bottles on the opening weekend. Eighty bottles of meatball. Why would people buy eighty bottles of meatball beer? Because unlike a market, you can't taste the beer first in a shop. You have to go on trust. These were people who had come in, seen a beer from the local area, decided to try and support a local business and consequently had their taste buds ruined for weeks.

I fell into a dangerous bout of depression. My nan's alarm clock returned once more and became a permanent fixture on the back of my eyelids. When I slept at night, great chunks of cliff were falling into the sea. I avoided people from the village. I avoided anyone with pursed lips, anyone who looked like they might have tasted a meatball beer. I began looking for other people to blame and finally I settled on all the other brewers who had ever existed. I blamed all the other brewers because beer shouldn't have to taste nice. That's not the point of beer. Indeed, it doesn't actually taste nice. If it wasn't alcoholic, we wouldn't drink it. If you've ever drunk a non-alcoholic beer you'll know exactly what I mean. On its own it's not a pleasant taste. It's the same as diet cola. Advertisers plead with you to drink diet colas, but you drink them and they're not pleasant. Our taste buds aren't as stupid as marketeers would like to believe. Our taste buds crave the bad stuff – the booze, the sugar, the fat, the X-rated bits. Our taste buds are sleazy. Our taste buds would hang out in strip clubs licking the ankles of table dancers if they could. It doesn't matter how stuck up you are, your taste buds are dirt.

I became obsessed with the idea that I shouldn't have to make a beer that tasted 'nice', because if brewers had stopped refining beer after inventing the first one, people would have been perfectly happy to drink it for eternity. Because they weren't drinking it for the taste, they were drinking it for its magic properties. They were drinking it for the alcohol, so the taste was irrelevant. But the problem was, over time some bastard decided to improve on the beer, even though it was serving its purpose, and that introduced relativity. One could compare one foul-tasting concoction to another slightly less foul-tasting concoction and, lo and behold, the taste of beer became important. And because of that, now I had to make something that tasted less foul than other beers. If some prick hadn't decided to continually improve the flavour of something that people were perfectly happy drinking, my beer would have gone down a storm at that market in Chaveignes. People would have treated my sweaty-balls beer that went to the farm shop as exactly what they were looking for, because it contained alcohol and that was what was supposed to be important. I was going insane.

As the pressure mounts you notice less and less around you. Your awareness becomes tunnelled, you lose peripheral vision and you notice only what is immediate.

The month wore on and I spent more time than usual in the brewery, but I wasn't really doing any brewing. I was just hanging around. I didn't want to brew any more.

It was my fortieth birthday in late November and Rose forced me to return to England to see my family. I'd often thought of celebrating my fortieth birthday in grand style, but when it came around I wasn't in the least interested in celebrating it. I wanted to be back in the brewery, not brewing beer, where I belonged. But it was a detour, a surprise on the way home that gave me some perspective.

I thought we were going straight back to Braslou from the UK but, unbeknownst to me, Rose had organised a weekend in a hotel on the Normandy coast, just to the west of Le Havre. When she told me, I couldn't bring myself to explain to her that I didn't really want to go, that I wanted to hide in my little brewery back in Braslou and wait till it was all over, so I tried to look pleased when we stopped up at this hotel by the sea in a place called Barneville.

At first, I hated it because there was so much I had to do back in Braslou. I'd left the brewery in a terrible state. My new fermenters were due to arrive. I had mountains of beer that tasted of sweaty balls to drink. But we walked on the beach every morning past Second World War concrete bunkers submerged in sand and we tried to convince each other how lucky we were not to be stuck in offices. I watched my son run around with the freedom of the whole beach, splashing in the sea in his little wellington boots and kicking and prodding little see-through inflatable cushions that were scattered all over the beach, which we assumed were seaweed.

It's very moving, the Normandy coast around Barneville – little crescent beaches, cliffs and coves. It's free of the expectations of nice weather, unlike the beaches on the west coast and in the South of France, which can seem glum and underwhelming unless it's a beautiful day. You can appreciate the beauty of a Normandy beach whatever the weather. Indeed, I think I prefer a Normandy beach in the rain because they have a melancholy that is comforting. Melancholy calms the mind. Just walking with Rose and watching Albert play, I knew I had to keep trying. I had to pick myself up and I had to keep trying, regardless of whether it seemed hopeless. You don't have a choice when there are people you love so much. Now I could see how far I had sunk into self-pity and I knew I had to rise out of it, whether I wanted to gently suffocate or not. I had to provide for Albert and keep him safe at all costs. That was the most important thing. I watched him kicking the little inflatable cushions up in the air and suddenly everything was in perspective. And then I remembered: there was still one more market at Marigny-Marmande. I must keep brewing beer because there was one more chance. I had to make this a success. It was about providing for my family. I needed to be a success so that I could provide for Albert. So that he could grow up in a loving, safe environment.

On passing through the foyer of the hotel we noticed a large sign showing a picture of one of the little inflatable cushions we'd seen on the beach with the writing: PORTUGUESE MAN O' WAR – VERY DANGEROUS. DO NOT TOUCH. I looked down at Albert. He had several of them skewered on a stick.

I'll always remember that weekend on the coast as a pivotal moment. A moment when I realised giving up wasn't an option. When I realised I had to persist. When I realised, thanks to some terrible parenting, our son almost got poisoned by a Portuguese man o' war. I emailed Jean Thomas to request a stand at the market in Marigny-Marmande. I was all in. I had to keep trying.

Two brand new egg-shaped fermenters, each a metre and a half tall, were waiting at the gates of La Ruche when we returned to Braslou. The cavalry had arrived.

BEER NO. 10:

Berger Blonde

RECIPE	MISTAKES
5.8 kg Pilsner malt	None
300 g Wheat	
100 g Menanoidin malt	
20 g Saaz hops 20g at 60 minutes	
15 g Huell Melon at 10 minutes	

December was cold. It rained relentlessly. The garden cut up and turned boggy. The fields around us were grey and barren, and the house that seemed so glamorous when the sun shone now looked glum and neglected. Gadget stumped round the field drenched through. Everything is more extreme here than it is in England. The hot weather is hotter, the cold weather is colder, the rain is heavier, the wind is ... well, you get the picture. The types of insects and reptiles you get are just a little more threatening. The further south you go, the more extreme it gets. We are not that far south, but compared to the UK, in Braslou it feels like you are a little closer to death.

Rose was back in England with Albert, seeing her family. I brewed again, this time for the market in Marigny-Marmande. My blonde beer, Berger Blonde, and my Clifton Porter. This time, more than ever, my sanitary practices were fastidious. Whenever I was about to take a shortcut I would force myself to think, *What would Monsieur Richard do?* And I would make sure I did it properly.

My recipes were refined. I reduced the wheat a little in the blonde to make it smoother. I added rolled barley to my Clifton Porter to make it thicker. The brews went well and when I pitched the yeast into the egg-shaped fermenters, within a day there was life. I did my best to control the temperature of the brewery using the only thing at my disposal, a paraffin heater. The brews fermented out in a week and I transferred them into a storage tanks, dry hopped the porter and left them to settle out and clear for a couple of days before bottling them.

We went for Sunday lunch at the Bergers in mid-December, a few days before the truffle market in Marigny-Marmande. I brought the Berger Blonde and the Clifton Porter to try. They weren't quite ready, but they were close. I had already tasted them, of course. They were bloody excellent.

'It's too sweet,' said Damien on tasting the Berger blonde.

'You've got to be fucking kidding me.'

'What was that?'

'It's supposed to be a little bit sweet, Damien.'

'I like it. It is a good beer. This would sell well.'

I got the impression he meant, 'This would have sold well if you hadn't shredded your reputation at Chaveignes.' But he didn't say it. And that he didn't ever say, 'If you'd just listened to me from the start . . .' summed him up. A lot of people wouldn't have been able to pass up a chance to score a few points like that.

I'd never describe myself as a fantastic brewer. The great brewers, the master brewers, spend years studying their craft. They are almost as much of a chemist as they are a brewer. They have an understanding of the processes and an attention to detail that I will never have. I knew I wasn't the world's greatest brewer, but when it came to making beer in your barn from some pretty rudimentary equipment, after nearly two years' practice I was finally turning out some genuinely good beer. It was beer with character. It was like Fred's red. It had something of the barn in it. It was too oxygenated perhaps, maybe it had bits of dead spider floating in it, but that was a good thing. It was proper, farmhouse beer made with heart.

We passed the afternoon walking in the forest with the Bergers and their horses, which followed on tethers, and all of a sudden I started to notice the little things around me again. As I pushed Albert's buggy through the sand I noticed wild boar tracks all around me and I noticed deer far away, moving silently beneath the oaks and the pines. I noticed the floor of the forest was covered in a thousand shades of moss, from peppermint to avocado green. And I noticed I was starting to lose Rose.

I noticed that despite living in this wonderful house in the countryside, with this forest opposite us and being surrounded by such charming towns, Rose had been forced to spend more and more time at home in front of a computer screen working at her internet marketing job, and less and less time doing what she came to do. Any spare moments she had were spent looking after Albert. She was

214

barely leaving the house, and consequently she was going on more and more trips to England. This wasn't the life I had promised her. I realised that unless I got this brewery right very quickly, there was a good chance that one day she was going to go back to England and not come back. I had been completely self-obsessed for the last year and I hadn't noticed her slipping away.

So it all came down to the market in Marigny-Marmande. One more chance. The market was held on a Thursday, which meant Damien couldn't help me because he had to work. I would be on my own at the mercy of the French. The beer was good now. What I needed was for the people of the Richelais to give me a second chance.

I know this is quite a heavy emotional bit, but I'm going to break out here because I've just had an idea for a book that I want to run past you: *One Thousand Shades of Moss*. It's a racy, soft-porn story for moss lovers. Extract:

Peregrine rubbed Tabatha's expansive bosom in a large circular motion, her skin so soft to the touch that it reminded him of a fresh patch of sphagnales in the autumn.

'Oh Peregrine, keep rubbing my bosom in a circular motion, you're relentless, like a hand-held whisk. You're like a Nutribullet. Oh yes, *yes*, YES, SPOROPHYTES!!!'

Phone call from Mishi: 'Listen, now, Tommy, the flat-bottomed boat has broken its tether. It was last seen floating past Montsoreau, where the Vienne joins the Loire. That's not why I'm phoning you. I need you to dig some holes in my lawn.'

'Oh. Right. The boat's gone where?'

'It's heading out to sea. Never mind that. It's not important. Can you dig the holes or not?'

'I can't I'm afraid, Mishi. I've got to prepare for the market.'

'OK sweetie. Completely understand. Now, you sound terribly miserable, but you know you're on to something there. Stick at it.'

That a dog would know how important a set of van keys was is completely beyond comprehension. And yet while I chased Burt around the dingly dell, my precious van keys dangling from the side of his mouth, dripping with saliva, I'm telling you, he knew exactly how important they were. At this point It was 7 a.m.

'BURT! FOR GOD'S SAKE DESIST!' I cried as he hurtled around the garden like a jet-propelled beanbag until eventually his obesity sided against him and he came to a halt. I wrestled the keys out of his mouth and got into the 1982 Peugeot J9 *pompier* van.

It's funny, you know, Burt smells of fast-food trucks and old people's homes and I honestly can't tell you why that is. Sometimes when he's asleep in front of the log burner I lie down next to him and hug him and listen to his heart thudding away and I wonder why he hates me.

Three quarters of an hour after I'd managed to retrieve my keys, Burt was staring at me from the passenger seat of the *pompier* van.

'Why don't you take the car?' said Rose, who was standing by the van, wrapping her arms around herself to keep warm.

'No, Rose. It will start. It just has to warm up. It's a work of art.'

'But you've been trying to start it for three quarters of an hour. And it's not a work of art – it's just an old van. At this rate you're going to miss the market.'

It was now quarter to eight on the morning of 21 December. It was D-day. The day of the truffle market at Marigny-Marmande. The rules say you have to be there by 8 a.m. or they can give your stand to someone else. It was the most important morning of my life, so of course the bloody Peugeot wouldn't start. Of course it wouldn't. As the days got colder, the van had become more and more temperamental, but forty-five minutes without starting was exceptional.

Rose gave up trying to reason with me and returned to the warmth of the house. I sat in the van in the pitch black. I couldn't take the car because that would mean all the doubters would have been right about the van, and as everyone knows, it's better to bollocks up your last chance of salvation than admit you were wrong about something you were clearly wrong about. Burt was still staring at me from the passenger seat. I thought he'd be furious at having to sit in a freezing cold, unmoving van for forty-five minutes, but when I summoned the courage to meet his glare he was actually just staring blankly at me. He'd gone beyond rage. It was just a look of *How the . . . I mean what the even fuck is this?*

After trying and failing to start the van, you have to give it a bit of time for the engine to drain, so the forty-five minutes that morning had been spent by turning the key, listening to the starter motor whirr for thirty seconds and then spending ten infuriating minutes drinking more coffee from a flask I had made myself that was supposed to last all day and letting the engine de-flood before I could try again.

I had fifteen minutes before I had to be at the market. I was in a caffeine-induced state of extreme tension. I was angry, wildly paranoid and incredibly anxious. If the van didn't work this time I would be too late for the market and that would be it. I pulled the choke out to the maximum length and turned the key. The van turned over perfectly well, but it was not catching. Fifteen seconds passed. It was still turning over. Thirty seconds. The engine was flooding. It wasn't going to work. Forty-five seconds. It was pointless now. Burt yawned. I should have stopped but somehow I couldn't release the key. I just kept going. A minute. It was turning over slower now. The battery was running out. I rested my head on the steering wheel. A minute and fifteen seconds. Burt scoffed and shook his head. I looked over at him smirking. I looked back to the steering wheel. I looked over again at him, still smirking. I looked back to the wheel. It was then I realised: he had bloody sabotaged van. That was it. He had been building up to this ever since he had arrived, and I don't know how he did it, but he he had sabotaged my van and he had completed his mission to ruin my life. It was too much.

'WHY DON'T YOU BLOODY LOVE ME, BURT?' I screamed. I lunged at him, ready to sort this out once and for all, Greco-Roman style, but as I took my hand off the key and before I could get him into a head lock, there was a great roar. A glorious roar of an engine I will always remember. A roar that in truth probably sounded more like a koala bear coughing on a bong but to me sounded like the opening chords to the greatest 1980s power ballad ever written ('What about Love' by the band Heart, if you were wondering). The van was alive. I put my hands back on the wheel.

'LET'S FUCKING DO THIS!' I screamed to Burt, who was utterly unimpressed as I slammed the van into first and we powered out of the gates, a great jet of slick black smoke trailing behind us. We wheeled left onto the road to Marigny-Marmande, tyres squealing, not even bothering to see if anything was coming. I had ten minutes to get to the market. Easy in a normal car, not so good in the velocity-shy Beast of Burgundy. It was still dark and it was incredibly foggy. Visibility was about twenty metres. It might not have been fog; it might have just been the black smoke from the van. That was immaterial. It was going to be a terrifying drive.

I hammered the van up to 70 kph. There was an otherworldly drone all around me – a drone of vibrating metal and things that were formerly metal but had since degraded. Caffeine coursed through my veins. The face of Bad-Life-Choices De Niro appeared in a cloud in front of me saying, 'Don't go above seventy.' I kept my foot down. We hit 80 kph. I could see virtually nothing ahead of me. The rear-view mirror shook so much that it seemed I was in the midst of an earthquake. I didn't care. I kept my foot down. The speedometer continued to rise. If anything had stopped in the fog on the road ahead of me – a car, a bike, a wild animal – it would have been squashed flat, such was the lack of visibility combined with the ridiculous braking distances of the 1982 Peugeot J9 *pompier* van. 85 kph. The needle continued to rise. The noise was unbearable. I KEPT MY FOOT DOWN. Suddenly, as the noise in the van reached the point where it could go no further and its only option was to explode, the drone subsided and all I could hear was the gentle purring of the engine. The speedometer read 90 kph. The van stopped shaking.

The van loved 90 kph. That was its spiritual home. All this time I had been hacking around at 70 kph, worried that any faster and the van would explode, but in fact all it wanted to do was drive at 90 kph. The fog cleared. The van had reached some kind of state of bliss. Everything was OK. For a moment I didn't feel like my eyes were going to pop out.

We floated along the winding road from Braslou to Marigny in this old van, Burt, my faithful hound, glowering as a truly biting wind poured through the gaps in the doors and windows, as if we were being transported by a higher power, until finally we saw the light of the *salle des fêtes* – the village hall – just as you enter Marigny-Marmande. I swerved into the car park. People dived for cover. I jumped out of the van and charged into the hall to find where my stand was. The main hall was reserved for truffle sellers: it was a truffle market, after all. The smell of truffle was overwhelming, ever so slightly nauseating. A man pointed me over to a big white marquee attached to the side of the hall where the non-truffle market stalls were.

It was hectic in there. The *commune* had provided the tables for the stands, which were currently being pushed around and argued over by stallholders. People carried boxes and dragged great refrigeration units on trailers, it was pandemonium. To a man in my state, on the edge of pyschosis, it was the perfect place to be. The scenes of chaos mirrored what was happening in my head.

Most of the other stands were on their way to being completed. After a bit of pushing about, I found the organiser, a nice guy with a handlebar moustache, who assured me he hadn't given my stand away. He showed me to my table – a surprisingly decent spot in the centre of the marquee.

The market was about to start and I wasn't nearly ready. I ran back and forth to the van unloading my stock, my little fridge to keep the tasting beers cold, carry cases, boxes, my banner, which I attached to the front of the table, innumerable other bits and bobs that are necessary at a market stall. In the panic I didn't even have the time to worry about the significance of this market, about whether I had any reputation left, whether I would sell a single bottle of beer or instead be cast out by the people of the Richelais.

Finally, I had set up my beers and I was ready. A jolly-looking man with a grey beard came over and tapped me on the shoulder. He was very amused about something. He talked very quickly and I couldn't understand a word he was saying. I was too pumped up and flustered to be able to concentrate on him, I may as well have been on the phone to a fax machine, so I smiled and nodded furiously till he became confused and went away.

It felt busy from the start; there were people buzzing around behind me, people to the left and right of me, but no one seemed to be stopping at my stall. Now the enormity of what this market meant started to hit me. This was our future on the line. The future of my son. This was it . . . and nobody was stopping at my stand.

It was bizarre. The only way I could understand it was people must have been making a very deliberate choice to avoid my table. I mean, there was no one. Other stalls seemed to be doing brilliantly, but there was absolutely no one at my stall. My worst fears were realised. The damage had been done at the last market in Chaveignes and the sweaty-balls beer at the shop had finished me off. I must be a laughing stock. They must have organised this before I arrived. The people of the Richelais had organised a boycott of my beer. The shame alone was enough to mean we would have to leave Braslou, leave France, never mind the economic reality of having zero income. You can't keep making bad decisions and expecting everything to be OK. You can't sell people shit beer and expect them to forgive you. I might have made a few quid at that market at Chaveignes, but I'd finally pushed my luck too far and I'd lost people's trust.

My heart started to pound. I felt weak. I was suffering some kind of stroke. A heart attack, maybe. I didn't know what to do. I could feel the eyes of all the other stallholders staring at me. I pretended it was all fine for a few moments. Then I texted Rose: *We're fucked. I'm coming home. Also, I might be about to die of something.*

She replied: *OK, Tommy. We tried. Stay where you are. I'll come and buy some beer. Try and stay alive till then.*

I shut my eyes, dreading the appearance of my nan's alarm clock, but it wasn't there. Instead, I heared my nan saying to me, 'You're not facing life. You've got to face life.'

'I am facing life. There's nothing I can bloody well do, Nan.' I whispered to myself. As I said this, I realised the jolly guy with the grey beard was by my side again. This time he'd brought Sylvain, the pasta maker from the stall opposite, who I had met back at the asparagus market in Braslou. The jolly guy started rabbiting on and laughing again. I assumed he was trying to console me until Sylvain interjected.

'He's saying your stall is facing the wrong way.'

'What do you mean?' I didn't need this nonsense right now.

'The market is behind you. Look at the tables.' He said slowly and clearly.

I looked around. At first, I didn't understand what he meant. I was facing the main door where people entered. That seemed like a good direction to face. But as I looked at the table set-up, I realised that once all the tables had been erected they actually, very deliberately, formed a sort of passageway that snaked round the room. Customers had to follow this path. I was facing inwards, facing the backs of all the other stalls, standing in the gangway while the customers walked around behind me.

'Told you,' said my nan.

The jolly man burst out laughing and patted me on the back. He walked off, shaking his head. The other stallholders laughed. It was humiliating, but when you've made a fool of yourself as many times as I have, humiliation is a like an old friend. An old friend who you have tried to lose contact with, but who keeps finding out where you live.

I laughed weakly along with everyone else and set about turning my stand to face the right way. To face up to life. Thanks to the power of caffeine, within five minutes or so I was the other side of the table and my beers and banner were pointing in the right direction. It all made sense now – it was obvious, but at the time, when I had been setting up, not all the tables were erected, so you could walk in amongst the stands. Now people could only travel a certain way through the marquee. Suddenly there were customers at my stall. It was 9.30 in the morning. People were trying my beer!

I was told afterwards that the market wasn't as busy as it usually is, but I found it to be a whirlwind. A constant stream of people came to my stand and they were more enthusiastic than ever. It's a great feeling, selling something you are proud of. Most stallholders probably feel this from the beginning, because they're not idiot enough to ever try and sell something that they know is shit, but for me it was a new experience.

Mid-morning and Rose came to see how I was doing. It's fair to say she was surprised. She'd been expecting the worst.

'Are you OK? You seem to be doing all right,' she said, eyeing the great queue of people snaking from my stand.

'What? Oh, right. Yes. Sorry, Rose, false alarm. I just had my stand facing the wrong way, that's all. Simple mistake.'

'You did what? But surely only an absolute moron . . .?'

'Can't speak now, Rose, too many customers. I'll tell you about it later.'

The customers came in a steady stream throughout the morning. I was doing rather well. As far as I could see, the only person doing better than me was the guy next to me. He was selling snails. And as the market continued towards noon I did better and better.

The market ended suddenly about 12.30 p.m. and at last I had a chance to take stock. I had sold a lot of beer. In fact I had sold pretty much everything I had. Of course, I sold a lot of beer at Chaveignes and that had made me feel awful, but this was completely different. People genuinely liked the beer. I liked the beer. At Chaveignes, by selling shit beer I was making the world just a tiny bit worse. Now I was making the world better.

Relief doesn't generally rank at the top of the feelings

charts. It's normally happiness, bliss, ecstasy, those are the feelings that people associate with victory, but I felt relief. Glorious relief. It was mostly relief that my instincts were right. This was how it was supposed to have gone, this was how it had happened in my head right from the start. Despite each set back, my instincts were telling me that the brewery could work and I trusted them. This was just one market – I knew that, and there still issues to iron out – I had to iron out the problems with the van and of course I had to hit Burt really hard with an iron, but these were little problems. As the customers drifted away with bags of snails, truffles and beer I saw now that the opportunity to make this life sustainable was real. I had to make sure I took it, and if I did, I wouldn't have to go back to an office to die. And that was when I felt elated.

I swapped a bottle of beer for some spices with the lady behind me and another bottle for some fruit from the fruit and veg stand opposite. I swapped a beer for some of Sylvain's pasta and another bottle for a croissant and some bread. We all packed up and went in our different directions. The van started first time. On the journey home Burt stared at me blankly.

It was a cold winter but the house was warm. From the market on 21 December through to New Year I sold all of my stock. I removed all my meatball beer from the farm shop and sold only beer made from the new fermenters. Beer I was proud of. I sold hundreds of bottles at the farm shop. People were arriving every day at the brewery to buy beer. Lots of people who had tried it at the market. People who had heard about it from other people. I sold everything I had before the year was up. I knew then that if I could sell like this every month, I could make a living. We wouldn't be rich, but we could make enough between the two of us and Rose could spend more time making sculptures and less time sitting in front of a computer.

It was April. I had given in my notice to all my gardening clients because the brewery was a success. I strolled through the large barn doors into Rose's studio, having returned from my final ever gardening job. She was deep in concentration, finishing off a sculpture of a greyhound. I should have left her to it, but this was important.

'Rose, I've had the most extraordinary day! I've finally bonded with Burt!'

'What? But he hates you with every bone in his body.'

'His fat body, Rose. His fat body. That's what I thought, but listen to this. I was lying under a ride-on lawnmower at the bottom of the ditch next to Adrian and Suzannah's house.'

'You were doing what?'

'Yes, they'd warned me not to try and mow the grass along their drive with a ride-on lawnmower, but the alternative was to strim it and strimming takes much longer, and besides, whenever someone tells you not to do something, it could mean they're trying to hide buried treasure.'

'You've got to be kidding me,' said Rose.

' ... So I went mowing along the ditch and within moments the whole thing turned to shit and I found myself trapped under the lawnmower. But then Burt, who had been sniffing round the underside of the car – I believe attempting to work out where the brake lines were – saw me in peril and, much to my surprise, galloped over to me. As I lay there stricken, the weight of the lawnmower rendering me helpless, I fully expected Burt to use this opportunity to attack my face, but instead he sniffed around me, and then started licking me. And it was then I realised what Burt had been wanting all this time. I realised what Burt had been craving for. And he just wanted what all of us want, deep down.'

'Oh my God. He just wanted you to love him.'

'What? No, not love. God no. It's Burt. No, it was *croissants*. All this time he just wanted croissants. I was covered in croissant crumbs as usual. Little bugger licked me clean as a whistle. Some Eastern European vegetable pickers in the next field managed to lift the lawnmower off me.' (Let that be a lesson to you, Brexiteers.)

'Jesus. You've got to be more careful. You could have been killed.'

'Well look, Rose, it takes one to know one. So—'

'What does that mean? That doesn't make any sense at all. And how does that count as bonding with Burt anyway?'

'Don't you see? As long as I keep him fully stocked with croissants, he'll tolerate me.'

'But you can't keep feeding him croissants. He's practically obese anyway. It'll kill him.'

'But Rose, he'll tolerate me. Can't you see? He'll actually tolerate me!'

And that was how it played out. From then on, as long as I fed Burt some croissant every ten to fifteen minutes, he wasn't an arsehole.

So there you go. If you stick at something no matter what; if your motivation is the love and well-being of your family, and every time you face disaster it strengthens your resolve; if you are prepared to admit when you are wrong, prepared to learn from those around you, even the French, and prepared to gamble everything for what you believe, then perhaps one day an overweight hound might tolerate you, too.

BEER GLOSSARY

Hops – Plant distantly related to cannabis that provides bitterness, flavour and antibacterial qualities to beer.

Hot break – Foam formed of proteins that rise through the wort at the early stages of the boil.

Liquor – Brewing term: The water used to brew.

Malt – Grain that has been allowed to start germinatation before being kilned.

Mash – Soaking one's grains in water.

Sparging – Brewing term: Rinsing the grains of any remaining starch once the mash has finished.

Racking – Moving one's beer from the fermenter to a storage tank.

Trub – A bed of dead yeast and other bits.

Wort – Liquid full of sugar that is extracted from malt.

ACKNOWLEDGMENTS

I would like to thank the following people:

My wife, Rose, who stood alongside me through great tempests of uncertainty when others surely would have retreated to safety.

David Reynolds, for all his help both with the book and the brewery, and for being a good egg and a funny man. I owe him an enormous debt. Hopefully we can avoid the small claims court.

Maggi Healey, the first investor in the brewery and the saviour of Braslou Bière. Let's try and avoid the small claims court.

Aunty Myra and Uncle Chris, for reading everything I've ever written.

Sara Keane, who believed in me when I had all but given up. I will try and repay her faith. Ideally, we won't end up at the small claims court.

Damien and Celia, who took us in.

Emma Robinson and Shaun Walsh, who finally accepted my total ineptitude and set me free from the office.

Martha Reynolds, who gave me belief in my writing.

Chris Hosegood, who showed me that making mud coloured alcoholic liquids was possible.

Kate Quarry, the real talent.

Lastly, Sarah and Kate Beal – the greatest publishers of the 21st century. In an industry paralysed by fear it's extraordinary to meet people with a sense of adventure, with daring, courage and élan. I hope to repay their faith. I hope this means we can avoid the small claims court.